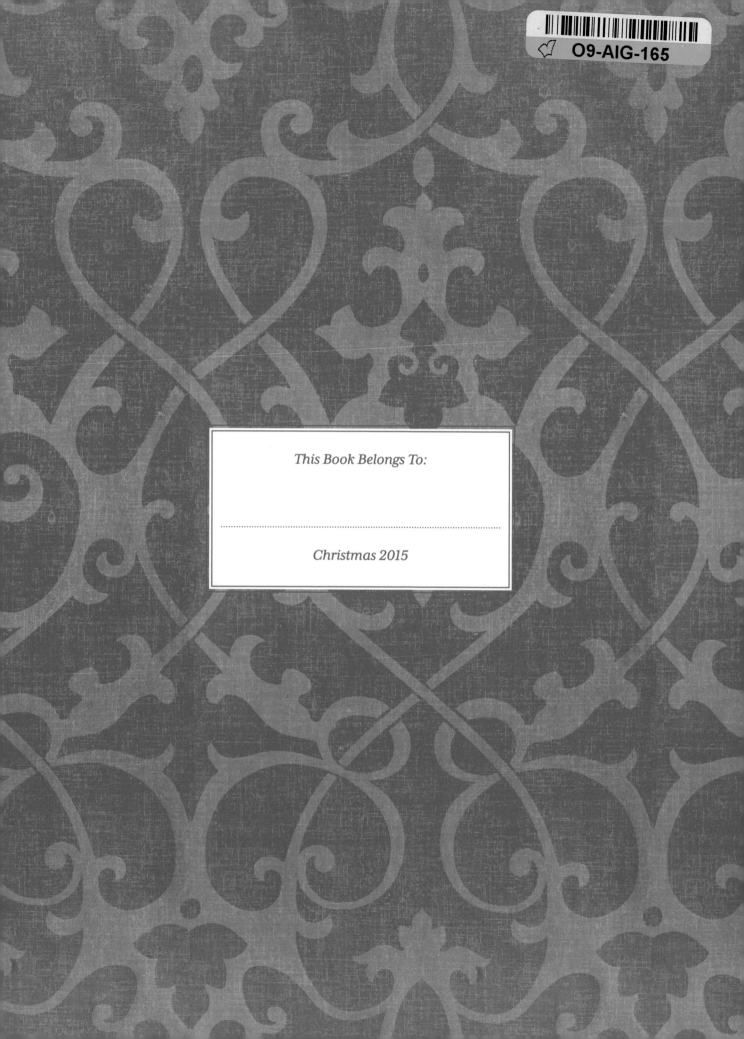

O9-AIG-165

This Book Belongs To:

....

Christmas 2015

2015
CHRISTMAS
—— WITH ——
Southern Living

2015
CHRISTMAS

— WITH —

Southern Living®

THE ULTIMATE GUIDE TO
HOLIDAY COOKING & DECORATING

Oxmoor
House®

Some of my best childhood memories revolve around the Christmas holidays—and not because of the presents we received (although my maternal grandmother was known to spoil her grandchildren incessantly). What I remember most about those days are the elaborate decorations and elegant dinners at my grandparents' home. The tree was always dressed to the nines with colorful bubbling tree lights (remember those?) and fabulous antique blown-glass ornaments. The staircase was draped in fresh garland, and vintage Annalee dolls climbed the banister and sat on the mantel just above where our family's handmade stockings hung. Christmas dinner was equally extravagant. We always enjoyed a standing rib roast with sautéed new potatoes, roasted onions, green beans, cornbread dressing, macaroni and cheese, and homemade biscuits. The annual spread was like no other during the year.

I treasure those times, and I hope they are the types of memories you'll be able to create with the help of this year's *Christmas with Southern Living*. The book is full of incredible party menus and decorating ideas (who doesn't want to re-create the Merry and Mod Cocktail Party on page 30), as well as tons of recipes to get you all the way through the holidays, from Christmas Eve to New Year's Eve. We've even included sweet and savory treats you can cook up and share as gifts with your friends and family.

So go and enjoy your Christmas, and I hope years from now what you'll remember about the holidays, too, are family, food, and fellowship—they are, after all, what the season is all about.

Sarah Gleim
Editor, *Christmas with Southern Living*

Contents

Entertain

SWEET HOME HOLIDAY

Nothing signals the holidays like a
traditional Southern Christmas dinner.
Surround yourself with friends and family
and make memories of a lifetime.

the menu

serves 8 to 12

GINGER-BOURBON SPARKLER

SPICY JOHNNY CAKES WITH SMOKED SALMON
AND LEMON CRÈME FRAÎCHE

GINGER AND BROWN SUGAR SMOKED
HOLIDAY HAM

SWEET POTATO PONE WITH
BOURBON AND BROWN SUGAR

CORN PUDDING WITH LEEKS AND THYME

BROWN BUTTER GREEN BEANS WITH
LEMON-PEPPER ALMONDS

CRANBERRY-HORSERADISH CHUTNEY

MOCHA PECAN PIE WITH
IRISH WHIPPED CREAM

COCONUT-PUMPKIN
CHIFFON PIE

GINGER-BOURBON SPARKLER

**MAKES 6 SERVINGS   HANDS-ON 6 MIN.
TOTAL 1 HR., 11 MIN.**

*This sparkling after-dinner drink is a perfect way to
end a sumptuous meal. The bitters and the ginger
act as digestives, and the bourbon warms you to your
toes. Be sure to buy a very dry sparkling white wine.*

½   vanilla bean, split
½   cup firmly packed brown sugar
½   cup chopped fresh ginger
¼   cup fresh lemon juice (2 lemons)
1   cup sparkling dry white wine
¾   cup bourbon
10   dashes of bitters
Garnishes: chopped pineapple, cranberries

1. Scrape seeds from vanilla bean pod. Bring vanilla
bean seeds, bean pod, brown sugar, ginger, and 1 cup
water to a boil in a medium saucepan; reduce heat,
and simmer, uncovered, 10 minutes. Remove from
heat; cover and let stand 20 minutes.
2. Pour ginger syrup through a fine wire-mesh sieve
into a bowl; discard solids. Let cool completely
(about 35 minutes).
3. Stir together ginger syrup, lemon juice, and
remaining ingredients in a pitcher. Serve over
ice in rocks glasses. Garnish, if desired.

SPICY JOHNNY CAKES WITH SMOKED SALMON AND LEMON CRÈME FRAÎCHE

MAKES 12 SERVINGS   HANDS-ON 17 MIN.   TOTAL 29 MIN.

These smoky, spicy bites of goodness make perfect starters to get your party going. Serve with a glass of Champagne.

2	cups stone-ground yellow cornmeal
¼	cup all-purpose flour
1¼	tsp. table salt
¼	tsp. ground red pepper
1	large egg, lightly beaten
1	cup milk
¼	cup unsalted butter, melted
1½	Tbsp. finely minced jalapeño pepper (½ pepper)
3	Tbsp. canola oil
½	cup crème fraîche
1	tsp. fresh lemon juice
¼	tsp. freshly ground black pepper
½	lb. thinly sliced smoked salmon, cut into 24 equal pieces
6	pickled okra pods, each cut diagonally into 4 pieces

Garnish: lemon zest

1. Combine first 4 ingredients in a large bowl. Whisk together egg, next 3 ingredients, and 2 Tbsp. water; whisk into flour mixture just until blended.

2. Heat 1 Tbsp. oil in a large nonstick skillet over medium-high heat. Drop ½ cup batter, by tablespoonfuls, 1 inch apart, into hot oil. Cook cakes 1 to 2 minutes on each side or until golden brown. Transfer cakes to a plate lined with a paper towel. Keep warm. Repeat procedure twice with remaining oil and batter.

3. Stir together crème fraîche, lemon juice, and black pepper in a small bowl until smooth.

4. Place cakes on a large serving platter. Place 1 salmon piece on top of each cake. Dollop cakes evenly with crème fraîche mixture, and top each with 1 piece of pickled okra. Garnish, if desired. Serve immediately.

GINGER AND BROWN SUGAR SMOKED HOLIDAY HAM

MAKES 12 SERVINGS
HANDS-ON 13 MIN.   **TOTAL 3 HR., 43 MIN.**

This holiday ham will be a hit with its bright ginger and mellow brown sugar flavors. There's plenty to feed a crowd, but if you are hoping for leftovers for sandwiches and meaty ham bone soup, there's plenty for that as well.

1	(15-lb.) smoked fully cooked, bone-in ham
42	(¼- x ⅛-inch) crystallized ginger pieces
1½	cups firmly packed light brown sugar
¾	cup ginger ale
½	cup whole grain mustard
2	Tbsp. apple cider vinegar
1	Tbsp. chopped fresh thyme

1. Preheat oven to 325°. Remove skin and excess fat from ham. Make shallow cuts in fat 1 inch apart in a diamond pattern. Make a small slit in center of each diamond; insert ginger pieces into slits.

2. Place ham on a rack in a large roasting pan. Pour water into roasting pan to a depth of ¼ inch. Cover top of ham loosely with aluminum foil. Bake at 325° for 2 hours and 40 minutes or until a thermometer inserted into thickest portion, not touching bone, registers 135°. Remove ham from oven. Increase oven temperature to 425°.

3. Stir together brown sugar and remaining ingredients. Brush 1 cup brown sugar mixture over ham. Bake, uncovered, at 425° for 40 minutes or until glazed and brown, basting every 10 minutes with remaining brown sugar mixture. Let stand 10 minutes before carving.

SWEET POTATO PONE WITH BOURBON AND BROWN SUGAR

MAKES 12 TO 15 SERVINGS
HANDS-ON 15 MIN.   **TOTAL 55 MIN.**

The sweet-and-savory flavors in this longtime favorite holiday dish will complement the saltiness of your smoked ham perfectly. This dish will also be convenient as a make-ahead side to save a little time for the hostess.

3	lb. sweet potatoes
6	Tbsp. unsalted butter, softened
1	cup firmly packed light brown sugar, divided
3	large eggs
6	Tbsp. bourbon
¾	tsp. freshly ground black pepper
1½	tsp. table salt, divided
6	Tbsp. butter, melted and divided
⅜	tsp. ground red pepper
1½	cups pecan pieces

1. Preheat oven to 375°. Peel and coarsely grate sweet potatoes to measure 8 cups, firmly packed.

2. Beat softened butter and ¾ cup brown sugar at medium speed with an electric mixer until fluffy. Add eggs, 1 at a time, beating well. Stir in bourbon, black pepper, and 1¼ tsp. salt. Stir in sweet potato.

3. Cook 3 Tbsp. melted butter in a 12-inch cast-iron skillet over medium-high heat until lightly browned. Add sweet potato mixture, spreading to edges of skillet. Increase heat to high, and cook, uncovered, 1 minute or until steam begins to escape. Bake, uncovered, at 375° for 20 minutes.

4. Meanwhile, combine ground red pepper, remaining ¼ cup brown sugar, remaining 3 Tbsp. melted butter, and remaining ¼ tsp. salt in a medium bowl. Add pecans, tossing to coat.

5. Sprinkle pecan mixture over potato mixture, and bake, uncovered, 20 more minutes or until pecans are lightly browned.

CORN PUDDING WITH LEEKS AND THYME

MAKES 12 TO 15 SERVINGS
HANDS-ON 26 MIN.   TOTAL 1 HR., 16 MIN.

Add leeks and thyme to this traditional standby and you'll not only enhance the sweetness of the corn, but you'll also create a new family favorite for your holiday table.

Vegetable cooking spray

8	ears fresh corn, husks removed
3	small leeks
4	applewood-smoked bacon slices
1	cup chopped sweet onion
¼	cup all-purpose flour
1	cup heavy cream
¾	cup half-and-half
2	tsp. chopped fresh thyme leaves
2	tsp. chopped fresh parsley
½	tsp. table salt
¼	tsp. freshly ground black pepper
4	large eggs, beaten
1	(8-oz.) package shredded Monterey Jack cheese

1. Preheat oven to 375°. Lightly grease a 13- x 9-inch baking dish with cooking spray. Cut tips of corn kernels into a large bowl; scrape milk and remaining pulp from cobs. Remove and discard root ends and dark green tops of leeks. Cut leeks in half lengthwise, and rinse thoroughly under cold running water to remove grit and sand. Coarsely chop leeks.

2. Cook bacon in a large skillet over medium heat until crisp; drain, reserving drippings in skillet. Sauté leeks and onion in hot drippings over medium-high heat 6 minutes or until tender. Sprinkle flour over onion mixture; cook, stirring constantly, 1 minute. Whisk in cream and half-and-half; cook, stirring constantly, 2 to 3 minutes or until thickened. Remove from heat. Cool slightly.

3. Stir thyme and next 4 ingredients into corn. Stir in onion mixture and cheese. Pour corn mixture into prepared baking dish. Bake at 375° for 45 minutes or until set and golden. Let stand 5 minutes before serving.

BROWN BUTTER GREEN BEANS WITH LEMON-PEPPER ALMONDS

MAKES 12 SERVINGS
HANDS-ON 10 MIN.   TOTAL 1 HR., 11 MIN.

Green beans are a favorite staple at the holiday table. These get a boost of flavor and lemony crunch from crispy almonds that can also double as a snack.

Parchment paper

1	large egg white
½	lb. sliced almonds
1	Tbsp. sugar
1	tsp. kosher salt
1	tsp. ground coriander
1	tsp. freshly ground black pepper
½	tsp. lemon zest
1½	lb. haricots verts (French green beans), trimmed
¾	cup butter
3	Tbsp. fresh lemon juice
¼	tsp. table salt
¼	tsp. freshly ground black pepper

1. Preheat oven to 275°. Line a large rimmed baking sheet with parchment paper. Whisk together egg white and 1 Tbsp. water in a large bowl until frothy. Add almonds, tossing to coat.

2. Combine sugar and next 4 ingredients in a large zip-top plastic freezer bag. Remove almonds from egg white mixture using a slotted spoon; place in bag. Seal bag, and shake until almonds are coated. Spread nuts, in a single layer, on prepared baking sheet.

3. Bake at 275° for 15 minutes. Toss gently, and bake 14 more minutes. Cool completely on pan on a wire rack (about 30 minutes). (Almonds will become crisp as they cool.)

4. Cook green beans in boiling water to cover 6 minutes; drain. Plunge beans into ice water to stop the cooking process. Drain and pat dry with paper towels.

5. Melt butter in a large skillet over medium heat. Cook 3 minutes or until butter begins to turn golden brown. Add beans, lemon juice, and next 2 ingredients. Cook 5 minutes or until beans are thoroughly heated, stirring often. Transfer beans to a large serving platter; sprinkle with desired amount of almonds. Serve immediately. Cover and store remaining almonds in an airtight container up to 1 week.

CRANBERRY-HORSERADISH CHUTNEY

MAKES 1¾ CUPS
HANDS-ON 17 MIN.   TOTAL 2 HR., 31 MIN.

This ruby-red chutney is a spectacular blend of sweet, tart, and savory flavors that will enhance your holiday meal.

½	vanilla bean, split
⅔	cup sugar
½	cup ruby port
1	(12-oz.) package fresh cranberries
¼	cup prepared horseradish

1. Scrape seeds from vanilla bean. Combine vanilla bean seeds, bean pod, sugar, port, and cranberries in a medium saucepan. Bring to a boil; reduce heat, and simmer 10 minutes or until cranberries burst and liquid is thick and syrupy. Remove from heat.

2. Remove and discard vanilla bean pod. Stir horseradish into cranberry mixture. Cover and chill 2 hours.

MOCHA PECAN PIE WITH IRISH WHIPPED CREAM

MAKES 8 SERVINGS
HANDS-ON 17 MIN.   TOTAL 7 HR., 52 MIN.

Rich flavors of chocolate and espresso intensify the ever-popular pecan pie. Topped with spiked whipped cream, this dessert is sure to be a hit among your friends and family.

1½ cups all-purpose flour
½   cup unsalted butter, cut up
2   tsp. kosher salt
¼   cup ice water
1   cup sugar
2   Tbsp. all-purpose flour
3   Tbsp. unsweetened cocoa
2   tsp. instant espresso
¼   tsp. table salt
1   cup light corn syrup
3   Tbsp. butter, melted
1   Tbsp. heavy cream
2   tsp. vanilla extract
3   large eggs, lightly beaten
1¼ cups chopped pecans
½   cup pecan halves
1   cup heavy cream
2   Tbsp. Irish cream liqueur
⅛   tsp. ground cinnamon

1. Preheat oven to 350°. Pulse first 3 ingredients in a food processor 8 times or until mixture resembles coarse meal. Add ice water, 1 Tbsp. at a time, and pulse until a dough forms. Shape dough into a disk. Wrap dough in plastic wrap, and chill 1 hour.

2. Roll dough into a 13-inch circle on a lightly floured surface. Fit piecrust into a 9-inch pie plate; fold edges under, and crimp. Chill 20 minutes.

3. Line pastry with aluminum foil, and fill with pie weights or dried beans. Bake at 350° for 15 minutes. Remove weights and foil, and bake 10 minutes or until dry and set, but not brown. Cool completely on a wire rack (about 40 minutes).

4. Whisk together sugar and next 4 ingredients in a medium bowl. Add corn syrup and next 4 ingredients; whisk until blended. Stir in chopped pecans. Pour filling into prepared crust. Carefully arrange pecan halves around edge of filling.

5. Bake at 350° for 1 hour and 10 minutes or until set, shielding edges with foil after 45 minutes to prevent excessive browning. Cool completely on a wire rack (about 4 hours).

6. Combine 1 cup heavy cream, liqueur, and cinnamon in a bowl; beat at high speed with an electric mixer until soft peaks form. Cover and chill until ready to serve. Serve pie topped with dollops of whipped cream. Sprinkle with extra cinnamon or nutmeg, if desired.

COCONUT-PUMPKIN CHIFFON PIE

MAKES 8 SERVINGS
HANDS-ON 35 MIN.   TOTAL 3 HR., 15 MIN.

This light and fluffy pie is traditional at its core, but sweet, nutty coconut adds a little something extra that will keep everyone coming back for more.

½   cup milk
2   envelopes unflavored gelatin
1   (15-oz.) can pumpkin
1   tsp. ground cinnamon
½   tsp. table salt
½   tsp. ground nutmeg
½   tsp. ground ginger
4   large pasteurized eggs, separated
1   cup plus 3 Tbsp. granulated sugar, divided
1¼ cups sweetened shredded coconut, divided
1   cup graham cracker crumbs
5   Tbsp. butter, melted
2   cups heavy cream
2   tsp. vanilla extract

1. Preheat oven to 350°. Whisk together milk and gelatin in a 3-qt. saucepan; let stand 1 minute. Cook over medium heat, stirring constantly, 1 minute or until gelatin dissolves. Stir in pumpkin, next 4 ingredients, egg yolks, and ½ cup sugar. Cook, stirring constantly, 5 to 7 minutes or until slightly thickened. (Do not boil.) Transfer to a bowl, and chill 40 minutes or to room temperature, stirring halfway through.

2. Meanwhile, place coconut in a single layer on a baking sheet, and bake at 350° for 8 to 10 minutes or until golden, stirring occasionally.

3. Stir together graham cracker crumbs, butter, 1 Tbsp. sugar, and 1 cup coconut. Press mixture into a 10-inch pie plate. Freeze 10 minutes or until ready to use.

4. Beat egg whites at high speed with a heavy-duty electric stand mixer, using whisk attachment, 8 minutes or until soft peaks form. Add ¼ cup sugar, and beat 2 to 3 minutes or until stiff peaks form.

5. Gradually fold egg whites into pumpkin mixture. Pour into crust. Chill 2 hours or until set.

6. Beat cream and vanilla at medium speed 1 to 2 minutes or until soft peaks form. Add remaining 6 Tbsp. sugar, and beat 1 to 2 minutes or until stiff peaks form. Top pie with cream mixture and remaining ¼ cup coconut. Serve immediately.

SEASON'S GREETINGS

Lush green swags of Fraser fir and boxwood garland
create graceful arches at the porch entry. A boxwood
kissing ball accented with red and white ribbon adds a
dose of whimsy that says "come on in!"

BECKON WITH BOUGHS AND BLOSSOMS

Create an enchanted entry with evergreen, boxwood, and flickering candlelight.

WISHES APLENTY

Letters to Santa are ready to go in a zinc mailbox embellished with flowers and a matching bow.

SCARLET ENDEAVOR

Force bulbs, like these amaryllis, right after Thanksgiving for perfect holiday blooms.

3

FRESH FOOTING

A burlap stocking with waterproof liner makes a surprising spot for cut flowers.

OH CHRISTMAS TREE

Turn to homespun accents, organic textures, and vintage finds to create a sweet Southern holiday scene full of nostalgia.

1 A freshly cut Fraser fir is the perfect shape for dressing up, plus it's native to the South. **2** Galvanized planters corral smaller packages while adding interest beneath the tree. **3** Small linen stockings accented with fabric and ribbon remnants can be filled with small surprises, too. **4** Stuffed fabric ornaments and balls wrapped in twine and yarn add to the homespun feel. **5** Simple, cut-alabaster ornaments glow when backlit with white lights.

RUSTIC IN RED

A vintage sled is a perfect decorative addition beneath the tree—it elevates gifts, putting the pretty wrapping center stage. Kraft paper, cardboard tags, garden twine, and a simple burlap tree skirt accented with reindeer combine to lend an easy, rustic feel to the decor.

MAKE A STATEMENT

A lush centerpiece is always eye-catching, but don't stop there. Decorate from top to bottom to make holiday entertaining extra special.

1

JINGLE BELLS

A spray of red berries and greenery graces chair backs embellished with red leather reindeer bells.

2

FESTIVE FLURRY

Red berries and greenery in faux snow-filled vases hang with snowflakes above the table.

3

RED, WHITE, AND PEWTER

A mix of patterns and materials creates a stylish, collected look.

"Carry Me Home
to See My Kin."
—Lynyrd Skynyrd, "Sweet Home Alabama"

MERRY AND MOD

Celebrate the season with classic cocktails and retro nibbles
that give a nostalgic nod to the festive and fabulous '50s.

the menu

serves 10

OLD-SCHOOL WHISKEY SOUR

CLASSIC DIRTY MARTINI

BOURBON-GLAZED SAUSAGE BALLS

DEVILED EGG TRIO

NOUVEAU RUMAKI

WARM TROPICAL CRAB BITES

SPICY THREE-PEPPER
PIMIENTO CHEESE LOG

GULF SHRIMP TOAST

"Nostalgia—it's delicate, but potent."

—Don Draper, *Mad Men*

OLD-SCHOOL WHISKEY SOUR

MAKES 1 SERVING
HANDS-ON 5 MIN.   TOTAL 5 MIN.

We recommend using your favorite bourbon in this traditional cocktail. Swap the basic maraschino cherry for Luxardo Italian maraschino cherries. You can purchase them online or at specialty foods stores.

¼ cup bourbon
2 Tbsp. fresh lemon juice
2 Tbsp. simple syrup
1 large pasteurized egg white (optional)
½ cup ice cubes

Combine first 3 ingredients and, if desired, egg white in a cocktail shaker; add ice cubes. Cover with lid, and shake vigorously until thoroughly chilled and egg white is foamy (about 30 seconds). Strain into a rocks glass filled with ice. Garnish with cherry and orange slice, if desired.

CLASSIC DIRTY MARTINI

MAKES 1 SERVING
HANDS-ON 5 MIN.   TOTAL 5 MIN.

Although the classic dirty martini uses gin as its base, this "tried-and-true" recipe gives the option for gin or vodka, depending on your preference. An atomizer is a great tool for evenly distributing a thin mist of vermouth in the glass and can be purchased at specialty stores or online.

½ tsp. extra dry vermouth
5 Tbsp. dry gin or vodka
1 Tbsp. Spanish olive juice
½ cup ice cubes
Garnish: large Spanish or other large green olives

Mist chilled martini glass with dry vermouth, or alternatively, add vermouth to glass and swirl to coat evenly. Combine gin (or vodka) and olive juice in a cocktail shaker; add ice cubes. Cover with lid, and shake vigorously until thoroughly chilled (about 30 seconds). Strain into chilled martini glass. Garnish, if desired.

BOURBON-GLAZED SAUSAGE BALLS

MAKES 44 MEATBALLS
HANDS-ON 15 MIN.   TOTAL 50 MIN.

These simple sausage balls with a bourbon-spiked peach glaze can be prepared ahead of time and reheated prior to serving. Keep them warm in a slow cooker, if you'd like.

2 (1-lb.) packages mild ground pork sausage
1 cup soft, fresh French breadcrumbs
⅔ cup finely chopped onion
2 large eggs, lightly beaten
2 tsp. grated fresh ginger
2 tsp. Worcestershire sauce
1 tsp. table salt
1 tsp. garlic powder
½ tsp. ground red pepper
2 cups peach preserves
¼ cup bourbon
2 Tbsp. apple cider vinegar
2 Tbsp. soy sauce

1. Preheat oven to 350°. Combine first 9 ingredients in a large bowl until blended. (Do not overwork meat mixture.) Shape mixture into 44 (1-inch) balls. Place sausage balls on 2 aluminum foil-lined 15- x 10-inch jelly-roll pans. Bake at 350° for 20 minutes or until meatballs are golden brown and no longer pink in center.

2. Meanwhile, combine peach preserves and next 3 ingredients in a Dutch oven. Cook over medium heat 5 minutes, stirring occasionally, or until preserves are melted. Place cooked sausage balls in sauce; cook on low heat 10 minutes, stirring occasionally.

DEVILED EGG TRIO

MAKES 18 SERVINGS   **HANDS-ON 50 MIN.**   **TOTAL 1 HR., 50 MIN.**

Deviled eggs, an ever-popular '50s cocktail party staple, are back in the limelight.
Here we offer an updated trio starring some of our test kitchen's favorite ingredients.

SMOKY BLT DEVILED EGGS

MAKES 6 SERVINGS
HANDS-ON 15 MIN.   **TOTAL 1 HR., 15 MIN.**

6	hard-cooked large eggs, peeled
3	hickory-smoked country bacon slices, cooked, divided
3	Tbsp. mayonnaise
1	Tbsp. minced green onions
1	tsp. Dijon mustard
1	tsp. apple cider vinegar
⅛	tsp. table salt

Pinch of ground red pepper

2	each, yellow and red grape tomatoes, sliced crosswise

1. Slice eggs in half lengthwise. Carefully remove yolks, keeping egg white halves intact, and place in a bowl.
2. Mash yolks until smooth. Finely crumble 1 bacon slice, and add to yolks. Stir in mayonnaise and next 5 ingredients until blended.
3. Spoon or pipe yolk mixture evenly into egg white halves. Cover and chill at least 1 hour or until ready to serve. Break remaining bacon into 12 pieces. Top egg halves evenly with bacon and tomato slices just before serving.

NOTE: We tested with Benton's Hickory-Smoked Country Bacon.

SMOKED PAPRIKA DEVILED EGGS WITH LOBSTER

MAKES 6 SERVINGS
HANDS-ON 15 MIN.   **TOTAL 1 HR., 15 MIN.**

6	hard-cooked large eggs, peeled
3	Tbsp. mayonnaise
2	Tbsp. minced celery
2	tsp. minced chives
1	tsp. Dijon mustard
½	tsp. lemon zest
1	tsp. lemon juice
¾	tsp. smoked paprika
⅛	tsp. table salt
12	small baby arugula leaves
1	Tbsp. olive oil, divided
1	(6-oz.) lobster tail, broiled or steamed

Garnish: chopped fresh parsley

1. Slice eggs in half lengthwise. Carefully remove yolks, keeping egg white halves intact, and place in a bowl.
2. Mash yolks until smooth. Stir in mayonnaise and next 7 ingredients until blended.
3. Spoon or pipe yolk mixture evenly into egg white halves. Cover and chill at least 1 hour or until ready to serve. Toss arugula leaves with 1 tsp. olive oil. Add salt and pepper to taste. Cut lobster meat into 12 pieces. Toss with remaining 2 tsp. olive oil. Toss with salt and pepper to taste. Top egg halves evenly with arugula and lobster just before serving. Garnish, if desired.

SRIRACHA-SPIKED DEVILED EGGS WITH GRILLED SHRIMP

MAKES 6 SERVINGS   **HANDS-ON 20 MIN.**   **TOTAL 1 HR., 20 MIN.**

6	hard-cooked large eggs, peeled
2	Tbsp. mayonnaise
1	Tbsp. Asian hot chili sauce (such as Sriracha)
1	Tbsp. minced green onions
1	Tbsp. minced fresh cilantro
1	small garlic clove, minced
1	tsp. fresh lime juice
1	tsp. rice vinegar
¼	tsp. table salt, divided

Vegetable cooking spray

6	peeled and deveined medium-size raw shrimp
2	tsp. olive oil
⅛	tsp. freshly ground black pepper

Garnish: fresh chives

1. Slice eggs in half lengthwise. Carefully remove yolks, keeping egg white halves intact, and place in a bowl.
2. Mash yolks until smooth. Stir in mayonnaise, next 6 ingredients, and ⅛ tsp. salt until blended.
3. Spoon or pipe yolk mixture evenly into egg white halves. Cover and chill at least 1 hour or until ready to serve.
4. Heat a cast-iron grill pan over medium-high heat. Coat pan with cooking spray. Brush shrimp with olive oil; sprinkle with pepper and remaining ⅛ tsp. salt. Cook 3 minutes or just until shrimp turn pink, turning once. Slice shrimp in half horizontally. Top egg halves evenly with shrimp. Garnish, if desired.

NOUVEAU RUMAKI

(pictured on page 36)

MAKES 10 SERVINGS
HANDS-ON 30 MIN.   TOTAL 1 HR., 30 MIN.

This twist on rumaki features Armagnac-soaked prunes filled with duck liver mousse pâté wrapped with pancetta. To dress up the occasion, serve these on a platter alongside Champagne grapes.

20	small dried pitted plums
¼	cup Armagnac or cognac
½	(7-oz.) package duck liver mousse pâté
20	walnut pieces, toasted
1	(3-oz.) package thin pancetta slices, halved crosswise
¼	cup ruby port
1	Tbsp. sugar
⅛	tsp. freshly ground black pepper

1. Bring dried plums and Armagnac to a simmer in a small saucepan over medium heat. Remove from heat; cover and let stand 1 hour.

2. Preheat broiler with oven rack 3 inches from heat. Drain dried plums, reserving any remaining Armagnac for another use. Cut duck liver mousse into 20 pieces. Cut a slit on 1 side of each dried plum with a sharp knife. Stuff 1 piece of duck liver mousse inside each dried plum. Top each mousse portion with a walnut piece. Wrap each dried plum in a half slice of pancetta. Place stuffed dried plums on an aluminum foil-lined broiler pan or sheet pan.

3. Bring port and next 2 ingredients to a simmer over medium-high heat. Cook 3 minutes or until reduced by half and mixture coats the back of a spoon.

4. Broil stuffed dried plums 2 minutes on each side or until pancetta is crisp. Let stand 2 minutes. Brush with port mixture. Serve immediately.

WARM TROPICAL CRAB BITES

(pictured on pages 36-37)

MAKES 12 SERVINGS
HANDS-ON 40 MIN.   TOTAL 40 MIN.

Our jazzed-up version of Crab Rangoon forgoes canned or imitation crabmeat in favor of fresh lump crabmeat and includes sweet mango, fresh ginger, and a kick of heat from serrano pepper.

¾	cup fresh lump crabmeat, drained
½	cup bottled sweet chili sauce
1	Tbsp. rice wine vinegar
1½	tsp. fish sauce
1	tsp. Asian chili-garlic sauce
½	(8-oz.) package cream cheese, softened
1	Tbsp. sour cream
¼	cup chopped green onions
1½	tsp. minced seeded serrano pepper
½	tsp. grated fresh ginger
¼	tsp. lime zest
1	small garlic clove, minced
Pinch of table salt	
¼	cup finely chopped mango
24	square wonton wrappers
1	large egg, lightly beaten
Parchment paper	
Vegetable oil	

1. Pick crabmeat, removing any bits of shell. Combine sweet chili sauce, next 3 ingredients, and 1½ tsp. water in a small bowl.

2. Stir together cream cheese and sour cream until smooth. Stir in green onions and next 5 ingredients. Gently fold in crabmeat and mango.

3. Place 1 wonton wrapper on a flat work surface. (Keep remaining wrappers covered with a damp towel to prevent drying out.) Spoon a generous 1½ tsp. crab mixture into center of each wonton wrapper. Lightly brush edges of wrapper with beaten egg. Bring all corners of the wonton together in the center to form a star shape, pressing seams gently to seal. Place on a baking sheet lined with parchment paper. (Keep filled wonton wrappers covered with a damp towel to prevent drying out.) Repeat procedure with remaining wonton wrappers, crab mixture, and egg.

4. Pour oil to depth of 3 inches in a Dutch oven; heat to 350°. Fry wontons, in batches, 1½ to 2 minutes on each side or until golden brown; drain on wire racks over paper towels. Serve with chili dipping sauce.

SPICY THREE-PEPPER PIMIENTO CHEESE LOG

(pictured on pages 36-37)

MAKES 24 SERVINGS
HANDS-ON 15 MIN. **TOTAL 4 HR., 15 MIN.**

This spicy pimiento cheese log, made with a combination of yellow and white Cheddars, is studded with jalapeño peppers, pimientos, chives, and bacon, and then rolled in toasted pecans. Serve with assorted crackers or crostini.

3 Tbsp. drained jarred diced pimiento
3 Tbsp. drained jarred diced pickled jalapeño peppers
2 Tbsp. grated sweet onion
2 Tbsp. minced fresh chives
¼ tsp. freshly ground pepper
1 (8-oz.) package cream cheese, softened
1 (8-oz.) block sharp Cheddar cheese, shredded
1 (8-oz.) block sharp white Cheddar cheese, shredded
1 (4-oz.) can diced jalapeño peppers, drained
8 bacon slices, cooked and crumbled
1½ cups chopped toasted pecans

1. Stir together first 9 ingredients in a large bowl. Stir in bacon.
2. Shape cheese mixture into 2 (9½-inch) logs; wrap in plastic wrap. Chill 4 hours or until firm.
3. Unwrap cheese logs and roll in pecans until evenly coated. Rewrap and chill if not using immediately.

holiday hints
MAKE AHEAD

Knock out the Spicy Three-Pepper Pimiento Cheese Log the day before your cocktail party. Mix all the ingredients, form the two cheese logs, wrap them in plastic wrap, and refrigerate right up until your guests arrive. Just before you set out your hors d'oeuvres, unwrap the cheese logs and roll them in pecans so the nuts stay crunchy. Serve and enjoy!

GULF SHRIMP TOAST

(pictured on pages 36-37)

MAKES 16 SERVINGS
HANDS-ON 35 MIN. **TOTAL 35 MIN.**

This rendition of the popular Chinese dim sum dish includes ground pork added to the Gulf shrimp mixture for extra flavor and is served with a hot mustard dipping sauce.

¼ cup Chinese-style hot mustard
1½ tsp. rice vinegar
1½ tsp. soy sauce
2 oz. ground pork sausage
1 tsp. cornstarch
10 oz. medium-size raw shrimp, peeled and deveined, divided
2½ Tbsp. finely chopped water chestnuts
2½ Tbsp. finely chopped green onions
1½ tsp. dark sesame oil
1½ tsp. Asian chili-garlic sauce
1½ tsp. soy sauce
1 tsp. grated fresh ginger
1 large egg, lightly beaten
8 thin white bread slices
Vegetable oil
Toasted sesame seeds

1. Whisk together first 3 ingredients and 2 Tbsp. water until smooth. Set aside.
2. Process sausage, cornstarch, and half of shrimp in a food processor until finely chopped, stopping to scrape down sides as needed. Add remaining shrimp, and pulse 15 times or until coarsely chopped.
3. Transfer shrimp mixture to a medium bowl. Stir in water chestnuts, next 5 ingredients, and 2 Tbsp. beaten egg, reserving remaining egg for another use.
4. Cut crusts from bread slices; cut each slice into 4 triangles. Spread 1½ tsp. shrimp mixture on each bread triangle.
5. Pour oil to depth of 2 inches in a Dutch oven; heat to 350°. Fry shrimp toasts, shrimp side down, in 6 batches, 2 minutes. Flip shrimp toasts over, and cook 1 minute or until golden brown; drain on wire racks over paper towels. Sprinkle desired amount of sesame seeds on top of mustard dipping sauce, and serve alongside shrimp toast.

WHITE CHRISTMAS

A flocked tree brings winter indoors and provides the perfect backdrop for mid-century flourishes in shades of shimmering blue, green, and copper.

GIFT TO BE TIED

Use gift wrap in coordinating colors and
retro patterns tied with a medley of ribbons
that fit the theme.

A RETRO HO-HO-HO

Space-age shapes and a subdued palette against a flocked tree add up to mid-century marvelous with ample doses of merry.

1

SHINE BRIGHT

A glittery star, with its clean lines and modern simplicity, is a nod to the Sputnik generation.

2

LAYERS OF LOVE

Holiday gifts add a decorative flourish and lots of anticipation beneath the tree.

3

BRIGHT COPPER

Rich taffeta ribbon glows beneath the tree and ties in with the copper ornaments hanging above.

LET IT SNOW

Snowflakes, starbursts, and icy branches
combine to make a showstopping tree.

FROSTY FLOWERBOX

A low, richly stained walnut box lends a masculine element to an arrangement of white anemones mixed with the muted blue and gray-green of brunia berries, dusty miller, and artemisia.

WINTRY SCENES ON EVERY TABLE

Inviting vignettes all around add interest and keep guests moving throughout the room to take it all in.

1 Geometric shapes—snowy alabaster statues and shimmering ornaments—mix with flowers to brighten the room. **2** Frost-kissed bottlebrush trees combine with modern wooden cutouts to add interest to a serving tray. **3** Flower-filled glass orbs and faux snow give an icy element to the table. **4** Wine is served from a vintage tiered stand flanked by a miniature forest. **5** White ranunculus and hydrangea rise like a snowdrift from this simple arrangement.

A CHRISTMAS STORY

Surprise little ones with a fanciful holiday
replete with all the trimmings and tasty treats
straight from the big-screen holiday classic. See if
you can find the nods to Ralphie's favorite...
and not-so-favorite...things.

the menu

serves 8 to 12

PINK BUNNY CUPCAKES

PEPPERMINT SWIRL HOT CHOCOLATE

MEATLOAF MUFFINS WITH
MASHED-POTATO TOPS

GREEN PEA BB'S AND
GREEN BEAN RIFLE SALAD

PORK EGG ROLLS

SWEET-AND-SOUR CHICKEN WITH RICE

KRIS KRINGLE AND SPRINKLES

Pink Bunny Cupcakes and Peppermint Swirl Hot Chocolate topped with holiday sprinkles and sanding sugar are sure to cancel out visions of sugarplums and keep little (and big) people happy.

PINK BUNNY CUPCAKES

MAKES 15 SERVINGS
HANDS-ON 22 MIN.   TOTAL 1 HR., 15 MIN.

Pink bunnies may seem out of season at Christmas, but these cute cupcakes are reminiscent of Ralphie's bunny costume his aunt Clara makes especially for his Christmas present. The batter is quick, simple, and doesn't require a mixer—but you can also use a box cake mix if you prefer.

CUPCAKES
15	paper baking cups
1	cup all-purpose flour
1	cup granulated sugar
½	cup unsweetened cocoa
1	tsp. baking soda
½	tsp. baking powder
½	tsp. table salt
⅔	cup buttermilk
½	cup canola oil
⅓	cup brewed coffee
½	tsp. vanilla extract
1	large egg

FROSTING
¾	cup butter, softened
3	cups powdered sugar
½	tsp. vanilla extract
1	to 2 tsp. whipping cream or milk

Pink gel paste food coloring
½	cup unsweetened finely shredded coconut

Vegetable cooking spray
8	marshmallows
2	Tbsp. light pink sanding sugar
15	toothpicks

1. Prepare Cupcakes: Preheat oven to 350°. Place paper baking cups in 15 regular-size muffin cups.

2. Whisk together flour and next 5 ingredients in a medium bowl. Whisk together buttermilk and next 4 ingredients; add to flour mixture, whisking until combined. Pour cake batter into cups, filling two-thirds full.

3. Bake at 350° for 18 minutes or until a wooden pick inserted in center comes out clean. Cool in pans on wire racks 5 minutes; remove from pans, and cool completely (30 minutes) on a wire rack.

4. Prepare Frosting: Beat butter at medium speed with an electric mixer until creamy. Gradually add powdered sugar, beating until blended. Add vanilla. Beat in desired amount of cream or milk until spreading consistency; beat in enough pink food coloring to tint frosting light pink. Spread or pipe frosting onto cupcakes. Sprinkle with coconut.

5. Coat scissors with cooking spray, and cut each marshmallow into 4 slices. Sprinkle cut sides of 30 slices with sanding sugar to resemble bunny ears. Break toothpicks in half; insert pointed ends of toothpicks about ½ inch into each of 30 marshmallow slices. Place 2 bunny ears on top of each cupcake by inserting the broken ends of toothpicks.

PEPPERMINT SWIRL HOT CHOCOLATE

MAKES 8 SERVINGS
HANDS-ON 27 MIN.   TOTAL 27 MIN.

Red-and-white-swirled peppermint-flavored whipped cream crowns this creamy hot chocolate for a twist on the candy cane theme.

2	cups milk
1	(12-oz.) can evaporated milk
3	cups heavy cream, divided
1	(12-oz.) package semisweet chocolate morsels
1	(10-oz.) package bittersweet chocolate morsels
½	tsp. vanilla extract

Pinch of salt
1	Tbsp. powdered sugar
½	tsp. peppermint extract
10	drops red gel paste food coloring

Marshmallows and candy sprinkles

1. Whisk together milks and 2 cups cream in a large saucepan. Cook, stirring constantly, over medium heat 15 minutes or until mixture comes to a boil. Reduce heat to low; whisk in chocolate morsels, vanilla, and salt until chocolate is melted and smooth. Keep hot.

2. Beat remaining 1 cup cream until foamy; add powdered sugar and peppermint extract, beating until soft peaks form.

3. Pour hot chocolate into 8 mugs. Insert a star-shaped tip into a large decorating bag; drop food coloring around inside of bag, allowing it to drip down sides. Carefully spoon whipped cream into bag. Pipe whipped cream onto hot chocolate; top each serving with a marshmallow or sprinkles. Serve immediately.

MEATLOAF MUFFINS WITH MASHED-POTATO TOPS

MAKES 12 SERVINGS
HANDS-ON 32 MIN.   TOTAL 1 HR., 17 MIN.

If your family members are cheese lovers, top the potatoes with shredded cheese before baking.

MEATLOAF

1½ Tbsp. olive oil
¾ cup finely chopped onion
¾ cup finely chopped carrot
3 garlic cloves, minced
Vegetable cooking spray
2¼ lb. extra-lean ground beef
1½ cups finely crushed bacon-flavored round buttery crackers (27 crackers)
¾ cup ketchup
1 tsp. table salt
2 tsp. Worcestershire sauce
¾ tsp. chopped fresh oregano
½ tsp. freshly ground black pepper
3 large eggs, beaten

MASHED POTATOES

1½ lb. Yukon gold potatoes, peeled and cut into 1-inch cubes
½ cup heavy cream, warmed
½ tsp. table salt
2 oz. Parmesan cheese, shaved
2 Tbsp. butter, melted

1. Preheat oven to 350°. Prepare Meatloaf: Heat oil in a large nonstick skillet over medium-high heat. Add onion and carrot; sauté 4 minutes. Add garlic; sauté 1 minute. Remove from heat, and cool completely (15 minutes).

2. Lightly grease 12 muffin cups with cooking spray. Combine ground beef, next 7 ingredients, and carrot mixture in a large bowl, using hands.

3. Spoon about ½ cup beef mixture into each prepared muffin cup. Bake at 350° for 35 minutes or until a thermometer inserted in center registers 160°. Remove meatloaf from oven. Increase oven temperature to broil.

4. Meanwhile, prepare Mashed Potatoes: Cook potatoes in boiling, salted water to cover 15 minutes or until tender; drain. Press potatoes through a ricer into a bowl. Stir in cream and remaining ingredients until smooth.

5. Insert a large metal star tip into a large decorating bag; fill with mashed potato mixture. Pipe potato mixture evenly onto meatloaves; drizzle with melted butter. Broil 6 minutes or until potato is golden brown. Remove from oven, and cool 5 minutes before serving.

GREEN PEA BB'S AND GREEN BEAN RIFLE SALAD

MAKES 12 SERVINGS
HANDS-ON 35 MIN.   TOTAL 35 MIN.

You won't shoot your eye out with this colorful side to our Meatloaf Muffins. Fresh or frozen, these green veggies will be sure to please those picky eaters.

1 cup (¼-inch) carrot slices
5 cups frozen peas
1¾ cups (3-inch) pieces green beans
½ cup plain Greek yogurt
1½ tsp. minced shallots
3 Tbsp. olive oil
2½ Tbsp. grated Parmesan cheese
½ tsp. freshly ground black pepper
½ tsp. finely chopped fresh dill
½ tsp. lemon zest
¼ tsp. kosher salt

1. Cook carrot in boiling water to cover in a Dutch oven 5 minutes. Add peas and green beans; cook 3 minutes or just until vegetables are tender. Drain and plunge into ice water to stop the cooking process. Let stand 1 minute. Drain; pat dry and place in a large bowl.

2. Process yogurt and next 7 ingredients in a food processor or blender until smooth. Add yogurt mixture to vegetables; toss well.

PORK EGG ROLLS

MAKES 10 SERVINGS
HANDS-ON 31 MIN.   TOTAL 41 MIN.

Homemade egg rolls are great finger foods for hungry kids. These are easy to prepare, and when served with a sweet teriyaki dipping sauce, they will disappear like magic.

1	lb. ground pork
1	tsp. dark sesame oil
2	cups angel hair slaw
1	cup grated carrot
¼	cup finely chopped green onions
½	tsp. grated fresh ginger
2	Tbsp. soy sauce
1	tsp. rice vinegar

Canola oil

10	egg roll wrappers
1	large egg, beaten
½	cup bottled sweet teriyaki sauce

1. Brown pork in a large nonstick skillet over medium-high heat, stirring often, 5 minutes or until meat crumbles and is no longer pink; drain. Transfer pork to a bowl. Heat dark sesame oil in skillet. Sauté slaw and next 3 ingredients in hot oil 3 minutes. Stir in soy sauce and vinegar. Add carrot mixture to pork in bowl; cool 10 minutes.

2. Preheat oven to 200°. Pour oil to depth of 2 inches into a Dutch oven; heat to 375°.

3. Meanwhile, working with 1 egg roll wrapper at a time, place wrappers diagonally onto a work surface (wrapper should appear diamond-shaped). (Keep remaining wrappers covered with a damp towel to prevent drying out.)

4. Spoon 3 Tbsp. filling into center of each wrapper. For each egg roll, fold top corner of each wrapper over filling; fold left and right corners over filling. Lightly brush remaining corner with beaten egg; tightly roll filled end toward remaining corner, and gently press to seal. Keep filled egg rolls covered with a damp towel until ready to fry.

5. Fry egg rolls, in 2 batches, 1 to 2 minutes on each side or until golden brown. Drain on a wire rack over paper towels. Place egg rolls on a baking sheet. Keep warm at 200° until ready to serve. Serve with teriyaki sauce on the side for dipping.

NOTE: We tested with Mr. Yoshida's Sweet and Savory Gourmet Sauce for the sweet teriyaki sauce.

SWEET-AND-SOUR CHICKEN WITH RICE

MAKES 4 SERVINGS
HANDS-ON 28 MIN.   TOTAL 28 MIN.

Crispy chicken bathed in a sweet sauce is a magnet for kids. If peppers are not a family favorite, substitute steamed broccoli.

Canola oil

1	cup all-purpose flour
½	tsp. garlic powder
¼	tsp. table salt
1	cup club soda
3	skinned and boned chicken thighs (½ lb.), cut into 2-inch pieces
1	skinned and boned chicken breast (½ lb.), cut into 2-inch pieces
2	Tbsp. firmly packed light brown sugar
2	tsp. cornstarch
½	cup canned pineapple juice
½	cup lower-sodium fat-free chicken broth
6	Tbsp. ketchup
5	Tbsp. rice vinegar
2	Tbsp. soy sauce
½	cup (1-inch) pieces onion
1	red bell pepper, cut into 1-inch pieces
1	green bell pepper, cut into 1-inch pieces
2	tsp. dark sesame oil
2	garlic cloves, minced
1½	cups (¾-inch) pieces fresh pineapple
2	cups hot cooked jasmine rice

Garnish: chopped green onions

1. Preheat oven to 200°. Pour oil to a depth of 3 inches into a Dutch oven; heat to 375°.

2. Combine flour, garlic powder, and salt in a medium bowl; make a well in center of mixture. Add club soda to flour mixture, stirring just until moistened.

3. Dip chicken pieces into batter, shaking off excess. Fry chicken in 2 batches, 2 minutes on each side or until golden brown. Drain on paper towels. Transfer to a baking sheet; keep warm at 200°.

4. Combine brown sugar and cornstarch in a bowl; stir in pineapple juice and next 4 ingredients.

5. Sauté onion and bell peppers in hot sesame oil in a large skillet over medium-high heat 4 minutes or until crisp-tender. Add garlic; sauté 1 minute. Reduce heat to medium. Stir in cornstarch mixture and pineapple. Bring to a boil; cook, stirring constantly, 1 minute or until thickened. Add chicken, stirring gently to coat. Serve over rice. Garnish, if desired.

"We plunged into the cornucopia quivering with desire and the ecstasy of unbridled avarice."

—Ralphie, diving into gifts under the tree in *A Christmas Story*

FRINGE BENEFITS

Abundant strips of felt hide stocking surprises
beneath a simple evergreen garland topped
with faux snowballs and colorful pillar candles.

MANTEL AND TREE MAGIC

1 Vintage-inspired ornaments will make parents and grandparents smile. **2** A multicolored felt tree skirt, bright red ball-fringe ribbon, and Santa wrapping paper set a fanciful tone. **3** A present opened on Christmas Eve satisfies this Ralphie look-alike. **4** "It's a major award!" **5** A classic red woody topped with a tiny tree is a happy nod to the holidays. **6** It's hard to stay frosty by the roaring fire, but this little fella will make everyone merry. **7** An old-fashioned mercury glass tree ornament adds a bold geometric touch. **8** Red and white bowling pins reinforce the vintage vibe beneath the tree.

GIFTS GALORE

A metal rolling cart is like an indoor sleigh loaded with North Pole surprises ready for little hands to unwrap.

HIGH TEA AND TINSEL

Take a break from the holiday bustle, and gather for an afternoon tea Downton Abbey-style. Pull out all the stops—shine the silver, press the linens, decorate every nook and cranny, and light a roaring fire—for a high-style celebration that sets the tone for the season.

the menu

serves 6 to 8

STRAWBERRY-PEACH CHAMPAGNE

SALTED CHOCOLATE-BOURBON TRUFFLES

BROWN SUGAR-PECAN BUTTONS

SWEET MINT TEA

WARM BRIE TARTLETS WITH SPICED
APRICOT CHUTNEY

ORANGE-GINGER POPPY SEED MINI MUFFINS

BACON-WHITE PIMIENTO CHEESE
TEA SANDWICHES

CINNAMON-SUGAR SCONES WITH
MASCARPONE CREAM

STRAWBERRY-PEACH CHAMPAGNE

MAKES 8 SERVINGS
HANDS-ON 14 MIN.   **TOTAL 2 HR., 29 MIN.**

Turn your afternoon tea into a Champagne tea with this fruit-infused drink. Use a good-quality Champagne or dry Prosecco for the best flavor.

½   cup granulated sugar
½   cup sliced fresh strawberries
2   tsp. fresh lemon juice
2   ripe peaches, peeled and cut into 1-inch pieces
1   (750-ml.) bottle Champagne or sparkling wine, chilled

Garnish: sliced strawberries

1. Combine first 4 ingredients and 1 cup water in a small saucepan. Bring to a boil; remove from heat, and let stand 15 minutes. Process peach mixture in a blender until smooth. Pour peach mixture through a sieve into a bowl; discard solids. Cover and chill at least 2 hours.
2. Combine 2 cups syrup and Champagne in a pitcher, reserving remaining syrup for another use. Pour Champagne mixture into 8 Champagne flutes. Garnish, if desired.

SALTED CHOCOLATE-BOURBON TRUFFLES

MAKES 2½ DOZEN
HANDS-ON 28 MIN.   **TOTAL 4 HR., 28 MIN.**

Change the flavor of these by substituting your favorite liqueur for the bourbon. Whiskey, brandy, or coffee liqueur would also work well.

12   oz. semisweet chocolate, chopped
3   Tbsp. unsalted butter
1   tsp. vanilla extract
⅓   cup heavy cream
3   Tbsp. bourbon
⅛   tsp. sea salt
Unsweetened cocoa
Powdered sugar
Chocolate wafer cookies, finely ground
Wax paper

Combine first 3 ingredients in a large microwave-safe bowl. Heat cream and bourbon in a small saucepan over medium heat 3 to 4 minutes or until mixture is hot but not boiling. Pour cream mixture over chocolate. Let stand 1 minute.

2. Stir chocolate mixture until melted and smooth. (If mixture doesn't melt completely, microwave at HIGH 30 seconds.) Stir in sea salt. Cover and chill 3 hours or until firm. (Mixture can be prepared and chilled up to 2 days ahead.)
3. Shape mixture into 1-inch balls (about 2 tsp. per ball). Roll in cocoa, powdered sugar, or finely ground chocolate wafers, as desired. Place on wax paper-lined baking sheets. Chill 1 hour.

BROWN SUGAR-PECAN BUTTONS

MAKES 1½ DOZEN
HANDS-ON 11 MIN.   **TOTAL 59 MIN.**

These buttons are a cross between a traditional shortbread and a wedding cookie, but the addition of brown sugar makes them a chewy, buttery treat.

Parchment paper
1   cup butter, softened
⅓   cup firmly packed light brown sugar
3   Tbsp. granulated sugar
2¼   cups all-purpose flour
⅓   cup finely chopped toasted pecans
1   cup powdered sugar
2   Tbsp. milk

1. Preheat oven to 325°. Line a baking sheet with parchment paper.
2. Beat butter and sugars at medium speed with an electric mixer until fluffy. Gradually add flour and pecans, stirring well. (Dough will be slightly crumbly.) Pat or roll dough to ½-inch thickness on a lightly floured surface; cut with a 1½-inch round or fluted round cutter. Place on prepared baking sheet.
3. Bake at 325° for 23 minutes or just until bottoms are lightly browned. Cool 5 minutes. Transfer cookies to a wire rack, and cool completely (20 minutes).
4. Stir together powdered sugar and milk in a small bowl until smooth. Drizzle glaze over cookies.

SWEET MINT TEA

MAKES 6 SERVINGS
HANDS-ON 9 MIN.   TOTAL 14 MIN.

You can find Chinese gunpowder green tea at most specialty foods markets, although regular green tea will work just fine. This tea is also delicious served cold over ice.

½ cup mint leaves, crushed
5 Chinese gunpowder green tea bags
2 (3-inch) strips fresh lemon rind
⅓ cup sugar
Garnish: fresh mint sprigs

1. Bring 6 cups water to a boil in a medium saucepan. Remove from heat; add mint, tea bags, and lemon rind. Cover and steep 5 minutes.
2. Remove tea bags. Strain tea mixture through a fine wire-mesh sieve into a teapot or pitcher; discard solids. Stir in sugar until dissolved. Pour into tea cups. Garnish, if desired.

WARM BRIE TARTLETS WITH SPICED APRICOT CHUTNEY

MAKES 15 SERVINGS
HANDS-ON 33 MIN.   TOTAL 33 MIN.

Using prepared phyllo shells saves you time when making this sweet-and-savory chutney. Use any leftover chutney as a spread for sandwiches, or spoon over roasted chicken or pork chops.

2	(1.9-oz.) packages frozen mini-phyllo pastry shells, thawed
½	cup finely chopped onion
1	garlic clove, minced
1	Tbsp. olive oil
½	tsp. ground cinnamon
¼	tsp. table salt
¼	tsp. ground cumin
¼	tsp. ground coriander
1½	cups chopped dried apricots
⅓	cup raisins
¼	cup dried currants
⅔	cup firmly packed light brown sugar
¼	cup apple cider vinegar
1	(8-oz.) Brie round*

Garnish: chopped fresh chives

1. Place phyllo cups on a serving platter. Sauté onion and garlic in hot oil in a medium saucepan over medium-high heat until tender. Stir in cinnamon and next 3 ingredients; cook 1 minute. Add apricots, next 4 ingredients, and ½ cup water. Bring to a boil; reduce heat, and simmer 15 minutes or until thickened.

2. Trim and discard rind from cheese; cut into 30 (½-inch) pieces. Divide cheese pieces among phyllo shells; spoon about 1½ tsp. hot chutney over cheese in each tartlet, reserving remaining chutney for another use. Garnish, if desired. Serve warm.

* Camembert or cambozola cheese may be substituted.

ORANGE-GINGER POPPY SEED MINI MUFFINS

MAKES 2 DOZEN
HANDS-ON 8 MIN.   TOTAL 46 MIN.

These moist and delicious muffins are a perfect holiday gift from your kitchen as well as a welcome addition to your holiday brunch.

1	cup all-purpose flour
1½	tsp. baking powder
¼	tsp. baking soda
4	tsp. poppy seeds, divided
¾	cup buttermilk
⅓	cup firmly packed light brown sugar
¼	cup butter, melted
2	Tbsp. chopped crystallized ginger
1	large egg, lightly beaten
2½	tsp. orange zest, divided
Vegetable cooking spray	
1½	cups powdered sugar
3	Tbsp. orange juice

1. Preheat oven to 400°. Combine first 3 ingredients and 1 Tbsp. poppy seeds in a bowl; make a well in center of mixture. Combine buttermilk, next 4 ingredients, and 2 tsp. orange zest; add to dry ingredients, stirring just until moistened.

2. Coat 24 miniature muffin cups with cooking spray. Spoon batter into muffin cups, filling two-thirds full.

3. Bake at 400° for 8 minutes or until lightly browned. Immediately remove from pans. Cool completely on wire rack.

4. Stir together powdered sugar, orange juice, and remaining ½ tsp. orange zest in a small bowl until smooth. Dip tops of muffins into glaze, and sprinkle with remaining 1 tsp. poppy seeds. Let stand 10 minutes until glaze is set.

BACON-WHITE PIMIENTO CHEESE TEA SANDWICHES

MAKES 8 SERVINGS
HANDS-ON 25 MIN.   **TOTAL 25 MIN.**

As an alternate presentation, spread each slice of bread with the pimiento cheese mixture, sprinkle with bacon, and cut in half, creating an open-faced sandwich instead.

3	Tbsp. mayonnaise
1	(3-oz.) package cream cheese, softened
6	oz. sharp white Cheddar cheese, shredded
3	oz. fontina cheese, shredded
3	Tbsp. chopped green onions
½	tsp. Worcestershire sauce
¼	tsp. ground red pepper
¼	tsp. table salt
⅛	tsp. freshly ground black pepper
1	(4-oz.) jar diced pimientos, drained
16	thin white bread slices
6	hickory-smoked bacon slices, cooked and crumbled

1. Place mayonnaise and cream cheese in a medium bowl; beat at medium speed with an electric mixer until smooth. Stir in Cheddar cheese and next 6 ingredients. Fold in pimientos.

2. Cut crusts from bread slices. Spoon cheese mixture onto 8 bread slices. Sprinkle evenly with crumbled bacon; top with remaining 8 bread slices. Cut each sandwich diagonally in half.

CINNAMON-SUGAR SCONES WITH MASCARPONE CREAM

MAKES 8 SERVINGS
HANDS-ON 16 MIN.   **TOTAL 1 HR., 6 MIN.**

Traditional high tea often includes scones with clotted cream or Devonshire cream, which can be found mainly in specialty foods stores. Our recipe uses mascarpone cheese and whipping cream to mimic the thick, creamy, sweet topping that is the perfect accompaniment to a buttery scone.

	Parchment paper
2¼	cups all-purpose flour
⅓	cup granulated sugar
1	tsp. ground cinnamon, divided
1	Tbsp. baking powder
½	cup cold unsalted butter, cut into small pieces
2½	cups heavy cream, divided
1	large egg, lightly beaten
2	Tbsp. turbinado sugar
6	oz. mascarpone cheese
2½	Tbsp. granulated sugar
1	tsp. vanilla extract
¼	tsp. fresh lemon juice

1. Preheat oven to 425°. Line a baking sheet with parchment paper.

2. Whisk together flour, ⅓ cup granulated sugar, ½ tsp. cinnamon, and baking powder in a large bowl. Cut butter into flour mixture with a pastry blender until crumbly and mixture resembles small peas. Add 1 cup heavy cream, stirring just until dry ingredients are moistened.

3. Turn dough out onto a floured surface, and knead about 30 seconds or until smooth. Press or pat dough into a 7-inch circle.

4. Combine egg and 1 Tbsp. water in a small bowl; brush over tops of scones. Combine turbinado sugar and remaining ½ tsp. cinnamon in a small bowl; sprinkle over tops of scones. Cut round into 8 wedges. Place wedges 2 inches apart on prepared baking sheet.

5. Bake at 425° for 18 minutes or until lightly browned. Transfer scones to a wire rack; cool completely.

6. Combine mascarpone cheese, next 3 ingredients, and remaining 1½ cups cream in a medium bowl; beat at medium speed with an electric mixer until soft peaks form. Serve cream with scones.

"All this unbridled joy has given me quite an appetite."

—Violet Crawley,
Downton Abbey

CHINA AND SILVER

The holidays are the perfect time to bring out your finest china and linens. Sterling silver stays lustrous with regular use, so put it into action. A centerpiece of flowers and fruit is more elegant when arranged in a sterling silver bowl.

FORMAL AND FESTIVE

A blazing fire makes a formal sitting room an inviting spot for tea. Remnants of old Persian rugs find new life as stockings and a pillow. Ivory leather steamer trunks, the patina of fine silver, and ample doses of red lend a regal feel to the room.

REGAL WELCOME

Rich red accents mix with sparkling crystal and shimmering silver and gold to paint a stately picture just off the home's entryway.

CROWN JEWEL

A diminutive glittering crown adds a royal touch to the tree.

SPARKLING ACCENTS

Castoffs from an old chandelier, faceted crystals combine with beaded and golden ornaments for a bejeweled effect.

BERRY BURST

Bright red holly berry branches burst from a gilded crown, taking the place of the traditional star or angel.

FIR MAJESTY

Framed by puddling Champagne-colored silk drapery panels, this towering Fraser fir takes center stage in the dining room. Repeating the deep red, gold, and silver hues in ornaments, packages, and accents keeps things formal and festive.

HOLLYWOOD GLAM
NEW YEAR'S EVE

Ring in the New Year Roaring Twenties-style
with a sparkling cocktail party that
would make Gatsby proud.

the menu

serves 10

SPEAKEASY SPARKLER

SMOKED TROUT CANAPÉS

BEE'S KNEES COCKTAIL

PROHIBITION PUNCH

CRABMEAT COCKTAIL

ARTICHOKE CANAPÉS

HERBED LAMB CROSTINI

ASPARAGUS PARCELS

SPEAKEASY SPARKLER

MAKES 1 SERVING
HANDS-ON 5 MIN.   TOTAL 5 MIN.

Our Champagne sparkler gets a lift from moonshine and limoncello! These days you can purchase any number of fine bottles of handcrafted moonshine at your local package store.

1   sugar cube
Dash of lemon bitters
2½   Tbsp. moonshine
2   Tbsp. Italian lemon liqueur
⅓   cup Champagne or dry sparkling wine

1. Place sugar cube in a Champagne flute. Sprinkle sugar cube with lemon bitters.

2. Combine moonshine and liqueur in a cocktail shaker; add ice cubes. Cover with lid, and shake vigorously until thoroughly chilled (about 30 seconds). Strain into Champagne flute, and top with Champagne.

NOTE: We tested with Midnight Moon moonshine and limoncello for the lemon liqueur.

holiday hints

PIPE PERFECT!

Instead of spreading the crème fraîche onto the pumpernickel rounds for the Smoked Trout Canapés, spoon the mixture into a 1-qt. zip-top plastic freezer bag instead. Snip one corner of bag to make a small hole and then pipe the cream onto rounds. You can also insert a fluted piping tip for an even more dramatic presentation.

SMOKED TROUT CANAPÉS

MAKES 15 TO 20 SERVINGS
HANDS-ON 29 MIN.   TOTAL 1 HR., 44 MIN.

The simplicity of smoked trout on pumpernickel is given a Roaring Twenties-worthy elegance with horseradish-spiked crème fraîche and apple-cucumber relish.

½   cup crème fraîche or sour cream
2½   tsp. prepared horseradish
¾   tsp. lemon zest
Pinch of kosher salt
34   cocktail-size pumpernickel slices
½   cup finely chopped English cucumber
½   cup finely chopped peeled Granny Smith apple
⅓   cup finely chopped red onion
2   tsp. fresh lemon juice
1   tsp. rice vinegar
¼   tsp. kosher salt
⅛   tsp. freshly ground pepper
1   (8-oz.) package smoked trout, skin removed and flaked (about 1¾ cups)
Garnish: fresh watercress leaves

1. Combine first 4 ingredients in a small bowl. Cover and chill at least 1 hour.

2. Preheat oven to 350°. Cut pumpernickel slices into rounds using a 2-inch round cutter. Place rounds on a baking sheet. Bake at 350° for 15 minutes or until lightly toasted, turning once. Cool completely.

3. Combine cucumber and next 6 ingredients in a bowl. Top each pumpernickel round with a heaping ½ tsp. horseradish cream. Spoon trout evenly on top of horseradish cream. Top evenly with apple-cucumber mixture. Garnish, if desired.

BEE'S KNEES COCKTAIL

MAKES 1 SERVING   HANDS-ON 13 MIN.
TOTAL 1 HR., 13 MIN. (INCLUDING GINGER HONEY SYRUP)

Our version of this Prohibition-era cocktail includes a Ginger Honey Syrup and pineapple juice for a perfectly delightful New Year's sipper. This cocktail will have your guests returning for seconds!

- 3   Tbsp. dry gin
- 2   Tbsp. pineapple juice
- 2   tsp. fresh lemon juice
- 2   tsp. Ginger Honey Syrup
- ½   cup ice cubes

Garnish: fresh rosemary sprig

Combine first 4 ingredients in a cocktail shaker. Add ice cubes. Cover with lid, and shake vigorously until thoroughly chilled (about 30 seconds). Strain into a chilled coupe glass or other stemmed glass. Garnish, if desired.

GINGER HONEY SYRUP

MAKES 1 CUP
HANDS-ON 8 MIN.   TOTAL 1 HR., 8 MIN.

- ½   cup honey
- 1   (2-inch) piece fresh ginger, peeled and coarsely chopped

Combine honey, ginger, and ½ cup water in a small saucepan; bring to a boil, stirring constantly. Remove from heat; cool completely. Discard ginger. Transfer to a ½-pt. jar. Cover and chill 1 hour. Store in refrigerator up to 1 week.

PROHIBITION PUNCH

MAKES 1 SERVING
HANDS-ON 5 MIN.   TOTAL 5 MIN.

This swanky Champagne cocktail (which literally packs a punch) is a great way to get the celebration rolling.

3	Tbsp. brandy
2	Tbsp. cranberry juice cocktail
1	Tbsp. orange liqueur
2	tsp. fresh lemon juice
6	dashes of Peychaud's bitters
½	cup ice cubes
⅓	cup dry Prosecco or sparkling wine

Garnishes: lemon peel, sugared cranberries

Combine first 5 ingredients in a cocktail shaker. Add ice cubes. Cover with lid, and shake vigorously until thoroughly chilled (about 30 seconds). Strain into a chilled flute. Top with Prosecco. Garnish, if desired.

NOTE: We tested with Cointreau for the orange liqueur.

CRABMEAT COCKTAIL

MAKES 10 SERVINGS   HANDS-ON 23 MIN.
TOTAL 3 HR., 23 MIN. (INCLUDING PICKLED ONION)

Fresh lump crabmeat is given a tropical twist with fresh pineapple, cilantro, lime, and avocado. Dress up this hors d'oeuvre Gatsby-style by serving in cocktail glasses.

1	lb. fresh lump crabmeat, drained
1	cup finely chopped fresh pineapple

Quick Pickled Red Onion

5	Tbsp. fresh lime juice (about 3 limes)
3	Tbsp. chopped fresh cilantro
1½	Tbsp. olive oil
½	tsp. sea salt
¼	tsp. freshly ground black pepper
2	jalapeño peppers, seeded and minced
1	avocado, coarsely chopped

Garnish: lime wedges

1. Pick crabmeat, removing any bits of shell. Combine pineapple and next 7 ingredients in a large bowl. Gently fold in crab. Cover and chill thoroughly (at least 2 hours).
2. Fold in avocado just before serving. Divide crab mixture evenly among 10 martini or cocktail glasses. Garnish, if desired.

QUICK PICKLED RED ONION

MAKES ¾ CUP
HANDS-ON 7 MIN.   TOTAL 1 HR., 7 MIN.

¾	cup white vinegar
3	Tbsp. sugar
¼	tsp. table salt
1	(8-oz.) red onion, cut into thin half-moon slices and separated
½	cup ice cubes

Bring first 3 ingredients to a boil in a medium nonreactive saucepan over medium-high heat. Add onion; reduce heat to medium-low, and cook, uncovered, 1 minute. Remove from heat, and transfer to a bowl. Stir in ice cubes. Cover and chill thoroughly (at least 1 hour).

ARTICHOKE CANAPÉS

MAKES 23 SERVINGS
HANDS-ON 25 MIN.   TOTAL 1 HR., 15 MIN.

These Mediterranean-inspired canapés feature roasted artichoke hearts in a creamy goat cheese base and are topped with a fennel-olive relish.

1	small fennel bulb, sliced
1	(14-oz.) can quartered artichoke hearts, drained
1	(8.5-oz.) French bread baguette
¼	cup pitted kalamata olives, chopped
¼	cup pitted picholine olives, chopped
2	Tbsp. olive oil
2	tsp. lemon zest
⅛	tsp. dried crushed red pepper
1	(8-oz.) package cream cheese, softened
1	(4-oz.) goat cheese log, softened
2	tsp. chopped fresh thyme
2	tsp. fresh lemon juice
¼	tsp. table salt

Garnish: fresh dill sprigs

1. Preheat oven to 450°. Place fennel, in a single layer, on 1 side of a large rimmed baking sheet; place artichokes on opposite side of baking sheet.
2. Bake at 450° for 20 minutes or until fennel is golden brown, turning once. Transfer fennel to a cutting board and cool completely (10 minutes). Return artichokes to oven, and bake 10 more minutes or until lightly browned. Cool completely (10 minutes).
3. Reduce oven temperature to 350°. Cut baguette into 46 (¼-inch-thick) round slices; arrange slices in a single layer on a baking sheet. Bake at 350° for 10 minutes or until slightly golden. Cool completely (5 minutes).
4. Finely chop fennel. Combine fennel, olives, and next 3 ingredients in a small bowl.
5. Chop artichoke hearts. Stir together cream cheese and next 4 ingredients in a medium bowl until smooth. Stir in artichoke hearts.
6. Spread about 2 tsp. cream cheese mixture on each bread slice, and top each with about 1 tsp. fennel-olive relish. Garnish, if desired.

HERBED LAMB CROSTINI

MAKES 18 SERVINGS
HANDS-ON 22 MIN.   TOTAL 2 HR., 2 MIN.

Slow-roasted tomatoes with preserved lemon and harissa-spiked yogurt provide the perfect foil for succulent herbed lamb loin.

4	cups grape tomatoes
2½	tsp. kosher salt, divided
1¼	tsp. freshly ground pepper, divided
3	Tbsp. olive oil, divided
2	Tbsp. chopped preserved lemon peel
½	cup plain yogurt
1	Tbsp. bottled harissa
1½	Tbsp. chopped fresh thyme
1½	Tbsp. chopped fresh rosemary
3	garlic cloves, minced
5	lamb tenderloins (1 lb.)
36	round baked pita crackers

Garnish: fresh thyme leaves

1. Preheat oven to 250°. Arrange tomatoes in a single layer on a rimmed baking sheet. Sprinkle with ½ tsp. salt and ¼ tsp. pepper; drizzle with 1 Tbsp. olive oil, tossing to coat.

2. Bake at 250° for 1 hour and 30 minutes or until tomatoes are softened yet moist, turning every 30 minutes. Transfer tomatoes to a bowl; lightly mash with a fork, leaving some tomatoes whole. Stir in preserved lemon peel.

3. Stir together yogurt and harissa in a small bowl. Cover and chill.

4. Combine thyme, next 2 ingredients, remaining 2 tsp. salt, and remaining 1 tsp. pepper in a bowl. Stir in 1 Tbsp. olive oil. Rub herb mixture over lamb.

5. Heat remaining 1 Tbsp. olive oil in a large heavy skillet over medium-high heat. Cook lamb in hot oil 2 minutes on each side for medium-rare, or until desired degree of doneness. Remove lamb from skillet, and let stand 5 minutes.

6. Cut lamb crosswise into ¼-inch-thick slices. Spoon 1 Tbsp. tomato mixture onto each pita cracker. Top each with 1 lamb slice and ¾ tsp. yogurt mixture. Garnish, if desired.

NOTE: We tested with Sensible Portions baked pita crackers.

ASPARAGUS PARCELS

MAKES 20 SERVINGS
HANDS-ON 20 MIN.   TOTAL 34 MIN.

Asparagus spears, wrapped in prosciutto and phyllo pastry, get a bright tang from lemon-caper vinaigrette.

Parchment paper
1½	lb. fresh asparagus (60 thin spears)
2	Tbsp. chopped drained capers
1	tsp. lemon zest
2	Tbsp. fresh lemon juice
¼	tsp. table salt
¼	tsp. freshly ground black pepper
1	cup olive oil, divided
½	(16-oz.) package frozen phyllo pastry, thawed
10	thin slices prosciutto, halved

1. Preheat oven to 450°. Line a large baking sheet with parchment paper. Snap off and discard tough ends of asparagus. Combine capers and next 4 ingredients in a bowl. Gradually whisk in ½ cup olive oil until blended.

2. Unfold phyllo on a flat surface. Stack 4 sheets, brushing some of remaining ½ cup olive oil between sheets. (Keep remaining phyllo covered with a damp towel to prevent drying out.) Cut stack into 4 squares. (Keep squares covered with a damp towel to prevent drying out.) Repeat procedure with remaining phyllo sheets and remaining olive oil to form 20 squares.

3. Working with 1 square at a time, place 1 half slice of prosciutto on each square. Drizzle each slice with 1 tsp. lemon-caper vinaigrette. Place 3 asparagus spears on 1 side of each square; roll up jelly-roll style. Place rolls, seam side down, on prepared baking sheet.

4. Bake at 450° for 14 minutes or until phyllo is crisp and golden. Serve immediately with remaining ⅓ cup lemon-caper vinaigrette.

"And I like large parties. They're so intimate. At small parties there isn't any privacy."

—F. Scott Fitzgerald, *The Great Gatsby*

AULD LANG SYNE

Welcome the New Year and celebrate "times gone by" with a festive nod to the elegant touchstones of a romantic and roaring era. Add a touch of tinsel and faux snow, too.

● 1
GATSBY GLAM

A luxe classic car reminiscent of Gatsby's yellow Rolls-Royce graces the tree.

● 2
LITTLE FLAPPER

Perfectly at home in the tree, this sparkling sparrow is ready to party.

● 3
PINK AND GOLD

Trading traditional Christmas red for a dusty shade of pink adds retro flair.

ALL DRESSED UP
Dripping in tinsel and glimmering accents of silver and gold, the decor transitions from holiday to Happy New Year with zero effort.

PUTTIN' ON THE GLITZ

If ever there is a time to pull out all the stops, it's New Year's Eve.

①

VA VA ROOM

Drive home the old Hollywood glamour at every turn—from feathered flapper girls to sparkle and shine everywhere.

②

PUT SOME BLING ON IT

From rhinestone package toppers to strands of pearls on the tree, nothing is too over-the-top on New Year's Eve.

③

FIZZ AND FUR

Faux fur shrugs make great wraps for Champagne bottles. Gild the lily by adding a vintage brooch.

MANTEL MAGIC

A coral accent wall provides a rich backdrop for the mantel strung with glimmering garland and dressed with golden rock candy trees. Snowy fur stockings with sparkling stars are anything but traditional.

MIX AND MINGLE
A gold leaf-embellished tray and a metallic stand create a self-service dessert station.

HAPPY NEW YEAR!

Champagne on ice is always grand, but Champagne on diamonds is a girl's best friend.

'TWAS THE NIGHT BEFORE
Dinner

Leave the turkey and ham for
Christmas day, and prepare your family
a cozy dinner the night before.

DELTA TAMALES

MAKES 10 TO 12 SERVINGS
HANDS-ON 48 MIN.   TOTAL 11 HR., 5 MIN.

This popular Southern version of a classic Mexican dish can be found throughout Mississippi. And at no time are tamales more popular than during the holidays. Bring your family together to help assemble them.

2	Tbsp. chili powder
2	tsp. kosher salt
1	tsp. chipotle chile powder
1	tsp. ground cumin
1	tsp. smoked paprika
½	tsp. ground red pepper
1	(4-lb.) boneless pork shoulder roast (Boston butt)
1	medium onion, chopped
4	garlic cloves, minced
2	jalapeño peppers, seeded and minced
3	cups chicken broth
1	(6-oz.) package dried corn husks
½	cup vegetable oil
4	cups yellow cornmeal
2	tsp. baking powder
1	tsp. table salt
¾	cup lard, softened
1	(19-oz.) can enchilada sauce

1. Combine first 6 ingredients in a small bowl. Rub over pork. Place onion, garlic, and jalapeño pepper in a 6-qt. slow cooker. Place pork on top of vegetables. Pour chicken broth over pork. Cover and cook on LOW 8 to 10 hours or until pork is tender.

2. Soak corn husks in hot water 30 minutes or until softened. Drain husks, and pat dry.

3. Transfer pork to a large bowl; shred pork with two forks. Pour vegetable mixture through a wire-mesh strainer into another bowl. Stir cooked vegetables and oil into shredded pork, reserving cooking liquid for later use.

4. Whisk together cornmeal and next 2 ingredients in a large bowl; add lard. Gradually add about 2 cups reserved cooking liquid to cornmeal mixture, stirring until consistency of thick mashed potatoes. Discard remaining cooking liquid.

5. Spread 2 Tbsp. dough onto 1 side of each of 32 husks, leaving a 1-inch border around edges. (Keep remaining dough covered while filling each tamale to prevent drying out.) Spoon 2 Tbsp. pork mixture down center of dough. Fold long sides of husks over filling to completely enclose pork mixture with dough; fold up bottoms of husks over folded sides (leave top ends open). Place tamales on a baking sheet.

6. Stand tamales, open end up, in a steamer basket for a large Dutch oven. Pour water to depth of 2 inches into Dutch oven. Place steamer basket inside Dutch oven. Place a layer of remaining corn husks over tamales. Cover Dutch oven; bring water to a boil over high heat. Reduce heat, and simmer 1 hour and 30 minutes or until dough is firm and husks pull easily away from dough.

7. Cook enchilada sauce in a small saucepan until thoroughly heated; serve with tamales.

SHRIMP AND GOUDA GRITS

(pictured)

MAKES 8 SERVINGS   HANDS-ON 47 MIN.
TOTAL 47 MIN., INCLUDING GRITS

Using the rendered fat from the sausage to sauté the vegetables brings a smoky, spicy flavor to the dish.

8	oz. andouille sausage, sliced
1	medium onion, chopped
1	medium-size red bell pepper, chopped
1	medium-size green bell pepper, chopped
4	garlic cloves, minced
2	lb. medium-size raw shrimp, peeled and deveined
2	tsp. Creole seasoning
2	Tbsp. all-purpose flour
1	cup chicken broth
½	cup dry white wine
	Gouda Grits
¼	cup chopped fresh parsley

Cook sausage in a large skillet over medium-high heat 6 minutes or until browned. Remove from skillet with a slotted spoon. Add onion and peppers to pan; sauté 5 to 8 minutes or until tender. Add garlic; sauté 30 seconds. Stir in shrimp; sprinkle with Creole seasoning and flour, tossing to coat. Gradually stir in chicken broth and wine. Cook, stirring often, 4 minutes or until shrimp turn pink and sauce is slightly thickened. Stir in cooked sausage. Serve over Gouda Grits. Sprinkle with fresh parsley.

GOUDA GRITS

MAKES 8 SERVINGS   HANDS-ON 18 MIN.   TOTAL 18 MIN.

4	cups chicken broth
3½	cups milk
2	tsp. table salt
½	tsp. freshly ground black pepper
2	cups uncooked quick-cooking grits
6	oz. Gouda cheese, shredded
¼	cup butter

Bring first 4 ingredients to a boil in a Dutch oven over medium heat. Gradually whisk in grits. Reduce heat, and simmer, uncovered, 10 minutes or until thick, whisking often. Remove from heat; stir in cheese and butter, whisking until cheese melts.

SEAFOOD ST. JACQUES

MAKES 8 SERVINGS   HANDS-ON 20 MIN.   TOTAL 25 MIN.

Sweet shrimp and scallops in a velvety sauce are presented in beautiful scalloped shells for a perfect make-ahead dish you can pop under the broiler after an evening candlelight service. Round out the meal with crusty French bread and a green salad. It is perfect served with dry Champagne for holiday toasting.

1	lb. sea scallops
½	cup butter, divided
2	Tbsp. finely chopped shallots
1	Tbsp. finely chopped garlic
1	(8-oz.) package fresh mushrooms, thinly sliced
½	tsp. table salt
¼	tsp. freshly ground black pepper
1	cup dry white wine
1	lb. medium-size raw shrimp, peeled and deveined
¼	cup all-purpose flour
1	cup seafood stock
1	cup heavy cream
½	tsp. hot sauce, or to taste
	Vegetable cooking spray
2	Tbsp. finely chopped fresh parsley
⅛	tsp. ground red pepper
1	cup panko (Japanese breadcrumbs)
¼	cup grated fresh Parmesan cheese

1. Rinse scallops, and pat dry. Melt 3 Tbsp. butter in a large skillet over medium-high heat. Add shallots, garlic, and mushrooms; sauté 3 to 4 minutes or until tender. Stir in salt, pepper, and wine. Add scallops and shrimp; cover and cook 3 to 4 minutes or until shrimp turn pink and scallops are done. Transfer seafood and mushrooms to a bowl using a slotted spoon; reserve cooking liquid in skillet.

2. Add ¼ cup butter to reserved cooking liquid; cook over medium-high heat, whisking until butter melts. Whisk in flour until smooth. Add seafood stock, cream, and hot sauce; cook, whisking constantly, 5 minutes or until sauce is thickened. Remove from heat. Cool slightly.

3. Preheat broiler with oven rack 8 inches from heat. Lightly grease 8 (10-oz.) gratin dishes with cooking spray. Place dishes on a large baking sheet. Divide seafood mixture evenly among dishes. Spoon about ⅓ cup sauce over seafood mixture in each dish.

4. Place remaining 1 Tbsp. butter in a medium microwave-safe bowl. Cover and microwave at HIGH 1 minute or until butter melts. Stir in parsley and red pepper. Add panko and cheese; toss well. Sprinkle crumb mixture over seafood mixture.

5. Broil 4 minutes or until sauce is bubbly and tops are browned and crisp. Serve immediately.

MAKE-AHEAD: Cover and chill filled dishes up to 1 day ahead. Remove from refrigerator, and let stand 20 minutes. Sprinkle with crumb topping, and broil as directed in recipe.

CLASSIC BOUILLABAISSE WITH GARLIC CROUTONS

(pictured on page 98)

MAKES 8 SERVINGS
HANDS-ON 47 MIN.   **TOTAL 1 HR., 27 MIN.**

Bouillabaisse is a traditional Provençale stew, made with lots of different seafood and a flavorful, garlic-and-herb-infused broth. It's easy to prepare and perfect for Christmas Eve dinner.

1½	lb. unpeeled large raw shrimp
2	cups chopped sweet onion (1 large onion)
1½	cups sliced fennel (about ½ bulb)
1	cup sliced leek (1 leek)
⅓	cup olive oil
3	large garlic cloves, chopped
4	cups seafood stock
1	cup dry white wine
½	cup clam juice
⅓	cup chopped fresh parsley
2	tsp. kosher salt
½	tsp. freshly ground black pepper
¼	tsp. saffron threads
¼	tsp. dried crushed red pepper
1	(14.5-oz.) can diced tomatoes, undrained
1	lb. fresh mussels, scrubbed and debearded (about 13 mussels)
1	lb. littleneck clams in shells, scrubbed (about 14 clams)
1½	lb. grouper, cut into 1½-inch pieces
1	(16-oz.) sourdough bread baguette, cut diagonally into 16 slices
2	garlic cloves, peeled and halved
⅓	cup butter, melted

Chopped fresh parsley (optional)

1. Peel and devein shrimp, reserving shells.
2. Sauté onion, fennel, and leek in olive oil in a Dutch oven over medium-high heat 5 minutes or until tender. Add chopped garlic; sauté 2 minutes or until fragrant. Add seafood stock and next 8 ingredients; stir in reserved shrimp shells and 2 cups water. Bring to a boil; reduce heat, and simmer, uncovered, 30 minutes.
3. Preheat oven to 400°. Pour onion mixture through a fine wire-mesh strainer into a large bowl, pressing solids with the back of a spoon to release liquid. Discard solids. Return broth to Dutch oven. Bring to a boil over medium-high heat; add mussels and clams. Cover and cook 4 minutes or until shells just begin to open. Add shrimp and fish; cover and cook 6 minutes or until shrimp is done and fish flakes easily with a fork. Discard any unopened shells.
4. Place bread slices on a baking sheet. Bake at 400° for 6 minutes or until toasted. Rub one side of each crouton with cut side of garlic halves; discard garlic halves. Brush garlic side of each crouton with melted butter.
5. Ladle bouillabaisse into 8 bowls. Sprinkle with chopped fresh parsley, if desired. Serve with croutons.

SPICED LAMB KEBABS WITH POMEGRANATE GLAZE

MAKES 8 SERVINGS
HANDS-ON 1 HR., 7 MIN.   **TOTAL 2 HR., 37 MIN.**

Lamb is often on the menu during the Christmas season in the Middle East and the Mediterranean. Serve these spice-rubbed kebabs with couscous and grilled vegetables.

⅓	cup olive oil
¼	cup chopped fresh mint
2	tsp. ground cumin
1	tsp. ground coriander
1	tsp. ground cardamom
½	tsp. freshly ground black pepper
4	garlic cloves, peeled
1	tsp. table salt, divided
2	lb. boneless leg of lamb, cut into 1-inch pieces
16	(8-inch) wooden skewers
2¼	cups pomegranate juice
½	cup brandy
¼	cup honey
1	(3-inch) orange peel strip
¼	cup cold butter, cut up

1. Process first 7 ingredients and ¾ tsp. salt in a blender or food processor until smooth, stopping to scrape down sides as needed. Transfer to a large bowl. Add lamb, tossing to coat. Cover and chill at least 1½ hours or up to 4 hours.
2. Soak wooden skewers in water 30 minutes. Thread lamb pieces onto skewers, leaving a ¼-inch space in between pieces. Sprinkle kebabs with remaining ¼ tsp. salt.
3. Heat a grill pan over medium-high heat. Add kebabs, in 2 batches, to pan; cook 3 minutes on each side or until desired degree of doneness. Place on a serving platter; keep warm.
4. Bring pomegranate juice and next 3 ingredients to a boil in a medium saucepan over medium-high heat; reduce heat, and simmer, uncovered, 32 minutes or until syrupy and reduced to ⅔ cup. Remove from heat; discard orange peel. Add butter, stirring until melted. Drizzle sauce over kebabs before serving.

LASAGNA BOLOGNESE

MAKES 12 SERVINGS
HANDS-ON 40 MIN. TOTAL 3 HR., 44 MIN.

This luscious pasta dish is well worth the effort. Traditional lasagna Bolognese includes homemade spinach lasagna noodles, but we've taken a shortcut here with dried noodles. Make the Bolognese sauce up to two days in advance, if desired.

2	Tbsp. olive oil
1¼	cups finely chopped onion
¾	cup finely chopped celery
¾	cup finely chopped carrot
3	garlic cloves, minced
1	lb. ground chuck
½	lb. mild Italian sausage, casings removed
¼	cup tomato paste
2	(28-oz.) cans crushed tomatoes
½	tsp. freshly ground pepper
4	cups milk, divided
2½	tsp. kosher salt, divided
16	uncooked lasagna noodles
6	Tbsp. butter
6	Tbsp. all-purpose flour
⅛	tsp. freshly grated nutmeg
2½	cups (10 oz.) freshly grated Parmigiano-Reggiano cheese, divided

Vegetable cooking spray

1. Heat oil in a Dutch oven over medium heat. Add onion and next 3 ingredients; sauté 8 minutes or until vegetables are crisp-tender. Add beef and sausage; increase heat to medium-high, and cook, stirring often, 6 to 8 minutes or until meat crumbles and is well browned. Stir in tomato paste; cook 2 minutes. Stir in tomatoes, pepper, 1 cup milk, and 2 tsp. salt; bring to a simmer. Reduce heat to low, and simmer 1 hour and 30 minutes or until sauce is thickened and reduced to 9 cups, stirring occasionally.

2. Prepare noodles according to package directions. Drain and plunge into cold water to stop the cooking process; drain and layer on a baking sheet. Drizzle olive oil between layers to prevent noodles from sticking together.

3. Melt butter in a heavy medium saucepan over low heat; add flour, whisking until smooth. Cook, whisking constantly, 1 minute. Gradually whisk in remaining 3 cups milk; cook, whisking constantly, over medium heat 2 minutes or until thickened and bubbly. Add nutmeg, ½ cup cheese, and remaining ½ tsp. salt; cook, stirring constantly, until cheese melts and sauce is smooth. Remove from heat.

4. Preheat oven to 375°. Lightly grease a 13- x 9-inch baking dish with cooking spray. Spread about 1¾ cups Bolognese sauce in bottom of prepared dish. Layer 4 lasagna noodles over sauce. Top with about 1¾ cups Bolognese sauce, a scant 1 cup white sauce, and ½ cup cheese. Repeat layers 3 times, beginning with noodles and ending with cheese. Coat dull side of a large piece of aluminum foil with cooking spray. Cover casserole tightly with prepared foil, coated side down.

5. Bake at 375° for 40 minutes. Uncover and bake 20 more minutes or until noodles are tender and top is brown. Let stand 20 minutes before serving.

EASY CHRISTMAS MORNING
Breakfast

You can make most of these simple
breakfast dishes ahead so you'll have more
time to spend Christmas morning
opening gifts and enjoying family.

SPICY SOUTHWESTERN BREAKFAST CASSEROLE

(pictured on page 106)

MAKES 8 SERVINGS   **HANDS-ON 22 MIN.**
TOTAL 17 HR., 42 MIN., INCLUDING CHILL TIME

This make-ahead breakfast casserole gets a spicy kick from smoked hot chorizo sausage and red cherry peppers. Smoked chorizo can be found at most specialty grocery stores, or substitute with another variety of spicy smoked sausage.

8   Texas toast slices or other thick bread slices
1   (7.9-oz.) package smoked hot chorizo sausage,
      cut into ¼-inch slices
2   Tbsp. canola oil
1½ cups chopped onion
4   poblano peppers, chopped
⅔   cup chopped and drained pickled red cherry peppers
1   (10-oz.) can diced tomatoes and green chiles, drained
Vegetable cooking spray
4   oz. quesadilla cheese, shredded
4   oz. pepper Jack cheese, shredded
6   large eggs, lightly beaten
1½ cups milk
1   tsp. table salt
½   tsp. freshly ground black pepper
Garnishes: chopped fresh cilantro, chopped green onions,
      fresh salsa

1. Arrange bread slices in a single layer on a baking sheet. Let stand, uncovered, 8 to 24 hours.
2. Cook sausage in a large skillet over medium-high heat, stirring often, 4 minutes or until lightly browned and oil is released. Drain, reserving 1 Tbsp. drippings in skillet. Add oil to drippings; heat over medium-high heat until hot. Sauté onion and poblano peppers in hot oil 5 minutes or until tender. Stir in cherry peppers and diced tomatoes. Remove from heat.
3. Lightly grease a 13- x 9-inch baking dish with cooking spray. Cut bread into 1-inch cubes to measure 8 cups. Arrange cubes in prepared dish; top with onion mixture and sausage, and sprinkle with cheeses.
4. Whisk together eggs and next 3 ingredients in a bowl; pour over bread mixture. Cover and chill 8 to 24 hours.
5. Preheat oven to 350°. Let baking dish stand at room temperature 30 minutes. Uncover and bake at 350° for 45 minutes or until puffed and golden. Let stand 5 minutes before serving. Garnish, if desired.

CINNAMON ROLL WAFFLES WITH BANANAS FOSTER SAUCE *(pictured)*

MAKES 10 SERVINGS
HANDS-ON 20 MIN.   **TOTAL 20 MIN.**

Cinnamon roll waffles are so easy and have a wonderful, chewy texture. Top these with decadent bananas Foster sauce, and you have a perfect Christmas brunch treat. You can easily double the recipe if you have a large crowd.

2   (17.5-oz.) cans refrigerated jumbo cinnamon rolls
Vegetable cooking spray
1   cup heavy cream
½   tsp. vanilla extract
½   cup butter
1   cup firmly packed light brown sugar
⅓   cup dark rum
4   medium-size ripe bananas, sliced
1   cup walnuts or pecans, toasted and chopped

1. Preheat oven to 200°. Preheat a Belgian waffle iron to medium heat. Line a baking sheet with aluminum foil.
2. Separate cinnamon rolls; reserve icing. Lightly flatten each roll to ½-inch thickness with your fingers. Coat preheated Belgian waffle iron with cooking spray. Place 1 flattened roll in center of each cavity of waffle iron. Cook until golden brown and done. Transfer waffles to prepared pan. Keep warm in oven at 200°.
3. Beat cream, vanilla, and icing from 1 can of cinnamon rolls at high speed with an electric mixer until soft peaks form, reserving remaining container of frosting for another use. Cover and chill.
4. Melt butter in a large skillet over medium-high heat; add brown sugar, and cook, stirring constantly, 2 minutes or until sugar melts.
5. Remove from heat. Stir in rum, then carefully ignite the fumes just above the mixture with a long match or long multipurpose lighter. Let flames die down.
6. Return skillet to heat. Cook, stirring constantly, 2 minutes or until sauce is smooth. Add banana slices; cook 1 minute, turning slices to coat.
7. Top each waffle with about ⅓ cup banana sauce and a large dollop of whipped cream mixture. Sprinkle with nuts. Serve immediately.

NOTE: We tested with Pillsbury Grands Cinnabon Cinnamon Rolls.

CRANBERRY STREUSEL MUFFINS

MAKES 1 DOZEN   **HANDS-ON 5 MIN.**   **TOTAL 23 MIN.**

A muffin is always more delicious with a sweet, crumbly topping, and these highlight seasonal cranberries.

¼ cup firmly packed brown sugar
¼ tsp. ground cinnamon
2¼ cups all-purpose flour, divided
3 Tbsp. butter, softened
⅓ cup chopped pecans
⅔ cup granulated sugar
1 tsp. baking powder
1 tsp. baking soda
¼ tsp. table salt
1 cup frozen cranberries, thawed and coarsely chopped
1 cup buttermilk
⅓ cup butter, melted
1 tsp. vanilla extract
1 large egg
Vegetable cooking spray

1. Preheat oven to 400°. Combine brown sugar, cinnamon, and ¼ cup flour in a small bowl; add softened butter, rubbing with fingers until crumbly. Stir in pecans. Cover and chill.

2. Combine granulated sugar, next 3 ingredients, and remaining 2 cups flour in a large bowl. Stir in cranberries. Make a well in center of mixture. Whisk together buttermilk and next 3 ingredients; add to dry mixture, stirring until just moistened.

3. Lightly grease a 12-cup muffin pan with cooking spray. Spoon batter evenly into cups, filling three-fourths full. Sprinkle with streusel mixture, pressing gently to adhere.

4. Bake at 400° for 18 minutes or until a wooden pick inserted in center comes out clean. Cool in pan on a wire rack 5 minutes. Transfer muffins to wire rack. Serve warm or cool completely (about 20 minutes).

SAUSAGE-AND-CHEDDAR HOECAKES WITH FRIED EGGS AND TOMATO RELISH

MAKES 6 SERVINGS
HANDS-ON 48 MIN.   TOTAL 48 MIN.

Personalize breakfast with these savory cornmeal cakes topped with eggs the way your guests like them. Topping them with the fresh and flavorful relish adds texture and color to this hearty holiday offering.

½	lb. ground pork sausage
2	Tbsp. shortening
1½	tsp. table salt, divided
2	cups yellow cornmeal
½	cup milk
1	large egg, beaten
½	cup (2 oz.) shredded sharp Cheddar cheese
¼	cup olive oil, divided
2	cups grape tomatoes, chopped
¼	cup finely chopped sweet onion
2	Tbsp. chopped fresh parsley
1	Tbsp. chopped fresh garlic
¼	tsp. freshly ground black pepper
	Vegetable cooking spray
6	large eggs

1. Preheat oven to 200°. Line a baking sheet with aluminum foil.

2. Brown sausage in a large nonstick skillet over medium-high heat, stirring often, 6 to 8 minutes or until meat crumbles and is no longer pink; drain. Wipe skillet with paper towels.

3. Pour 3 cups boiling water over shortening in a large heatproof bowl, stirring to melt shortening. Stir in 1 tsp. salt and cornmeal. Stir in milk. Stir in 1 egg. Fold in cheese and sausage.

4. Heat 1 Tbsp. oil in nonstick skillet over medium-high heat. Spoon ¼ cup batter for each of 6 hoecakes into hot oil in skillet. Cook 3 minutes on each side or until golden brown. Repeat procedure twice with remaining batter and 2 Tbsp. oil. Keep hoecakes warm on prepared pan in 200° oven. Wipe skillet clean after cooking hoecakes.

5. Combine tomatoes, next 4 ingredients, ¼ tsp. salt, and remaining 1 Tbsp. oil in a bowl.

6. Heat nonstick skillet over medium heat. Lightly coat skillet with cooking spray. Gently break remaining 6 eggs, 3 at a time, into hot skillet; sprinkle evenly with remaining ¼ tsp. salt. Cook 2 to 3 minutes on each side or until desired degree of doneness.

7. Place 3 hoecakes on each of 6 plates. Top hoecakes on each plate with 1 egg and ⅓ cup tomato relish. Serve immediately.

MINI SAUSAGE AND SPINACH FRITTATAS

MAKES 1 DOZEN
HANDS-ON 10 MIN.   TOTAL 36 MIN.

These individual frittatas are the perfect grab-and-go Christmas morning breakfast or brunch. Serve with mixed fruit and toast.

	Vegetable cooking spray
½	lb. ground pork sausage
10	large eggs
¼	cup half-and-half
¼	tsp. table salt
¼	tsp. freshly ground black pepper
⅛	tsp. ground red pepper
1	cup chopped baby spinach
½	cup chopped drained bottled roasted red bell pepper
1½	cups crumbled feta cheese, divided
¼	cup chopped fresh parsley

1. Preheat oven to 375°. Lightly grease a 12-cup muffin pan with cooking spray. Brown sausage in a large skillet over medium-high heat, stirring often, 6 to 8 minutes or until meat crumbles and is no longer pink. Drain.

2. Whisk together eggs and next 4 ingredients in a large bowl. Layer cooked sausage, spinach, bell pepper, and 1 cup cheese evenly in prepared muffin cups. Pour egg mixture over layers.

3. Bake at 375° for 18 to 20 minutes or until set but not dry. Let stand 5 minutes. Remove frittatas from pan. Sprinkle with chopped parsley and remaining ½ cup feta cheese before serving.

CHERRY-ALMOND FRENCH TOAST CASSEROLE

MAKES 8 SERVINGS   **HANDS-ON 11 MIN.**
TOTAL 9 HR., 6 MIN., INCLUDING CHILL TIME

This make-ahead casserole will make your Christmas morning breakfast a breeze. Assemble the night before, and let it bake while your family opens presents.

Vegetable cooking spray
1   cup firmly packed brown sugar
⅔   cup all-purpose flour
1   cup sliced almonds
⅔   cup cold butter, cut into pieces
1   (1-lb.) loaf challah bread, ends trimmed
½   cup dried cherries, chopped
6   large eggs
2½   cups half-and-half
2   Tbsp. granulated sugar
½   tsp. ground cinnamon
¼   tsp. almond extract

1. Lightly grease a 13- x 9-inch baking dish with cooking spray. Combine brown sugar, flour, and almonds in a medium bowl. Cut butter into almond mixture with a pastry blender or fork until crumbly.

2. Cut bread into ½-inch slices. Layer half of bread in bottom of prepared dish. Sprinkle with cherries and half of brown sugar mixture. Top with remaining bread slices. Cover and chill remaining brown sugar mixture.

3. Whisk together eggs and next 4 ingredients. Pour over bread slices. Cover and chill 8 hours.

4. Preheat oven to 350°. Sprinkle remaining half of brown sugar mixture over casserole.

5. Bake, uncovered, at 350° for 45 minutes or until golden brown and set. Let stand 10 minutes before serving.

SCRAMBLED EGGS AND GRITS BAKE

MAKES 8 SERVINGS
HANDS-ON 27 MIN.   **TOTAL 1 HR., 2 MIN.**

This layered egg and grits casserole is a delicious way to start your holiday morning. Serve with a fresh fruit salad for a complete meal.

1   cup whipping cream
2   Tbsp. butter
1   tsp. table salt
½   tsp. freshly ground black pepper
⅔   cup uncooked quick-cooking grits
8   oz. Gouda cheese, shredded and divided
Vegetable cooking spray
2   large eggs
8   large kale leaves
1   Tbsp. olive oil, divided
1½   cups chopped red bell pepper
6   green onions, chopped
1   (6-oz.) package Canadian bacon, chopped
6   large eggs
½   cup milk

1. Preheat oven to 350°. Combine first 4 ingredients and 1⅔ cups water in a large saucepan. Bring to a boil; gradually whisk in grits. Reduce heat, and simmer 4 minutes or until tender, stirring often. Add ½ cup cheese, stirring until melted. Remove from heat; cool 15 minutes.

2. Lightly coat a 13- x 9-inch baking dish with cooking spray. Lightly beat 2 eggs, and stir into cooled grits mixture. Pour mixture into prepared dish. Bake at 350° for 20 minutes or until almost set and slightly puffed.

3. Meanwhile, trim and discard tough stalks from center of kale leaves; coarsely chop. Wash kale under cold running water; drain.

4. Heat 1½ tsp. oil in a large nonstick skillet over medium-high heat. Sauté kale in hot oil 4 minutes or until wilted and liquid evaporates. Remove from skillet. Heat remaining 1½ tsp. oil. Add bell pepper; sauté 4 minutes. Add green onions; sauté 1 minute. Stir in kale.

5. Sprinkle kale mixture, Canadian bacon, and remaining 1½ cups cheese over grits. Whisk together 6 eggs and milk; pour over kale mixture.

6. Bake at 350° for 25 minutes or until a knife inserted in the center comes out clean. Let stand 10 minutes before serving.

CHICKEN-AND-CHEESE MINI WAFFLE SANDWICHES

MAKES 10 SERVINGS
HANDS-ON 15 MIN.   TOTAL 15 MIN.

Pick up chicken strips or nuggets from your grocery store deli or your favorite fast-food restaurant. Frozen, cooked chicken strips can also work.

- 1   (10.9-oz.) package frozen mini waffles
- 2   Tbsp. butter, melted
- 5   fast-food fried chicken strips, quartered
- 1   (7-oz.) package cracker-size extra-sharp Cheddar cheese slices
- 5   cooked bacon slices, quartered
- ⅔   cup stone-ground mustard
- ⅓   cup mayonnaise
- ¼   cup maple syrup

1. Preheat oven to 400°. Brush waffles with butter. Bake waffles according to package directions.

2. Place chicken pieces on an ungreased baking sheet. Place 1 cheese square on top of each chicken piece, reserving remaining cheese for another use. Bake at 400° for 1 to 2 minutes or until cheese melts.

3. Top each of 20 waffles with 1 bacon piece, 1 chicken piece, and 1 waffle. Secure with a wooden pick.

4. Stir together mustard, mayonnaise, and syrup in a small bowl. Serve with sandwiches.

NOTE: We tested with Eggo Minis Waffles and Cracker Barrel Extra Sharp Cracker Cuts Cheese.

THE MAIN EVENT

Dinner

Nothing impresses like a superb Christmas dinner. No matter who is on this year's guest list, you'll find everything you need to please those around your holiday table.

DUXELLES-STUFFED PORK TENDERLOIN *(pictured)*

MAKES 8 TO 10 SERVINGS
HANDS-ON 45 MIN.   TOTAL 1 HR., 15 MIN.

Pork tenderloins are delicious when stuffed with a sautéed mushroom mixture then wrapped in prosciutto to ensure a moist interior. The rich Marsala cream sauce makes this an extra-special, holiday-worthy main.

2   shallots, chopped
2   Tbsp. olive oil
2   (4-oz.) packages assorted mushrooms, coarsely chopped
1¼   tsp. kosher salt, divided
1¼   tsp. freshly ground black pepper, divided
2   large garlic cloves, minced
1½   tsp. chopped fresh thyme
¼   cup chopped fresh parsley
½   tsp. firmly packed lemon zest
2   Tbsp. fine, dry breadcrumbs
2   (1¼-lb.) pork tenderloins
1   (4-oz.) package thinly sliced prosciutto
Vegetable cooking spray
½   cup Marsala
1   cup reduced-sodium fat-free chicken broth
¾   cup heavy whipping cream
Garnish: fresh thyme sprigs

1. Sauté shallots in hot olive oil in a large nonstick skillet over medium heat 2 minutes or until crisp-tender. Add mushrooms, ½ tsp. salt, and ½ tsp. pepper; sauté 7 minutes or until tender and liquid evaporates. Add garlic and thyme; sauté 1 minute. Remove from heat, and stir in parsley, lemon zest, and breadcrumbs. Cool completely.

2. Butterfly each tenderloin by making a horizontal cut into 1 side of pork, cutting to within ½ inch of other side. (Do not cut all the way through tenderloins.)

3. Unfold tenderloins, forming rectangles, and place each between 2 sheets of heavy-duty plastic wrap; flatten to ½-inch thickness using a rolling pin or the flat side of a meat mallet.

4. Preheat oven to 400°. Spread mushroom mixture evenly over tenderloins, leaving a ½-inch border. Roll up tenderloins, starting at 1 long side. Sprinkle tenderloins with ½ tsp. salt and ½ tsp. pepper. Place half of prosciutto, overlapping slices, on top of each tenderloin. Wrap prosciutto around tenderloins; secure with kitchen string at 2-inch intervals.

5. Lightly grease a roasting pan with cooking spray. Place tenderloins in pan. Bake, uncovered, at 400° for 30 minutes or until a meat thermometer inserted into thickest portion registers 145°.

6. Transfer tenderloins to a platter, and cover with aluminum foil. Let stand 10 minutes.

7. Meanwhile, bring Marsala to a boil in a medium saucepan over medium-high heat. Boil, uncovered, 6 minutes or until reduced by half, stirring occasionally. Stir in chicken broth; return to a boil. Reduce heat, and simmer 9 minutes or until reduced by half. Stir in heavy cream, and simmer 3 minutes or until slightly thickened. Stir in remaining ¼ tsp. salt and ¼ tsp. pepper. Serve sauce with pork. Garnish with fresh thyme, if desired.

CIDER-ROASTED PORK LOIN

MAKES 8 SERVINGS   HANDS-ON 28 MIN.   TOTAL 2 HR., 58 MIN.

Pork loin is perfect when marinated and roasted in apple cider. This recipe can easily be doubled for a large crowd, or it's perfect as is for an intimate holiday meal for six or eight.

2   cups apple cider
1   cup chicken broth
2   tsp. chopped fresh thyme
2   tsp. chopped fresh rosemary
3   garlic cloves, minced
1   (3-lb.) boneless pork loin
Vegetable cooking spray
¾   tsp. freshly ground black pepper
2   tsp. kosher salt, divided
2   Tbsp. olive oil
2   Tbsp. butter, softened
2   Tbsp. all-purpose flour

1. Combine first 5 ingredients in a shallow dish or large zip-top plastic freezer bag; add pork. Cover or seal, and chill 1 hour. Remove pork from marinade, reserving marinade.

2. Preheat oven to 400°. Lightly grease a roasting pan with cooking spray. Pat pork dry. Sprinkle pork with pepper and 1½ tsp. salt. Cook pork in hot olive oil in a large skillet over medium-high heat 2 minutes on each side or until browned. Place pork in prepared pan.

3. Bake at 400° for 1 hour and 15 minutes or until a meat thermometer inserted into thickest portion registers 135°, basting occasionally with reserved marinade. Remove from oven, and let stand 15 minutes or until meat thermometer registers 145°. Place pork on a serving platter. Cover and keep warm.

4. Bring remaining reserved marinade and remaining ½ tsp. salt to a boil in a saucepan over medium-high heat; boil 10 minutes or until reduced to 1½ cups, skimming foam from sauce, if needed.

5. Stir together butter and flour in a small bowl until a paste forms. Add paste to marinade, whisking until smooth. Bring to a boil; reduce heat, and simmer, uncovered, 5 minutes or until sauce thickens and coats the back of a spoon, stirring often. Cut pork into slices; serve with sauce.

CORNISH HENS WITH MEYER LEMON, FENNEL, AND OLIVES

MAKES 6 SERVINGS
HANDS-ON 36 MIN.   TOTAL 1 HR., 47 MIN.

1   cup picholine olives
1½ lb. small red potatoes, unpeeled and quartered
2   small onions, cut into ½-inch-thick wedges
1   medium fennel bulb, cut vertically into ½-inch-thick slices
3   Tbsp. olive oil
2¼ tsp. kosher salt, divided
1¼ tsp. freshly ground black pepper, divided
10 Tbsp. butter, softened
3   Tbsp. chopped fresh parsley
2   tsp. firmly packed Meyer lemon zest
3   garlic cloves, minced
6   (1¾-lb.) Cornish hens
3   Meyer lemons, each cut into 8 wedges
2   Tbsp. all-purpose flour
1½ cups chicken stock

1. Preheat oven to 425°. Combine first 4 ingredients in a large roasting pan. Drizzle with olive oil, and sprinkle with 1 tsp. salt and ½ tsp. pepper. Toss to coat, and spread vegetables in an even layer. Bake at 425° for 15 minutes.

2. Meanwhile, combine butter and next 3 ingredients. Reserve 2 Tbsp. butter mixture in a small bowl. Remove and discard giblets and necks from hens. Rinse hens and pat dry. Loosen and lift skin from breasts of hens with fingers (do not totally detach skin); spread remaining butter mixture underneath and on top of skin. Carefully replace skin.

3. Place 3 lemon wedges in the cavity of each hen; sprinkle hens with 1 tsp. salt and ½ tsp. pepper. Tie ends of legs together with kitchen twine. Place hens on top of vegetable mixture in roasting pan.

4. Bake, uncovered, at 425° for 1 hour and 6 minutes or until a meat thermometer inserted in thickest portion of thigh registers 165° and vegetables are tender. Transfer hens and vegetable mixture to a serving platter; cover loosely with aluminum foil. Reserve drippings in roasting pan.

5. Add flour to reserved 2 Tbsp. butter mixture, stirring until smooth. Place roasting pan over 2 burners on stove over medium-high heat. Add chicken stock and cook 3 minutes, stirring to loosen browned bits in bottom of pan. Whisk in flour mixture; cook, whisking constantly, 2 minutes or until thickened. Stir in remaining ¼ tsp. salt and remaining ¼ tsp. pepper. Serve gravy with hens and vegetables.

BOURBON-CIDER ROASTED TURKEY WITH BBQ GRAVY

(pictured on page 114)

MAKES 10 TO 12 SERVINGS   HANDS-ON 36 MIN.
TOTAL 11 HR., 56 MIN., INCLUDING CHILL TIME

Soaking your turkey overnight in this sweet brine will ensure you end up with tender, moist meat that is full of flavor. If you'd rather skip the barbecue flavor in your gravy, simply leave out the barbecue sauce.

1½	cups kosher salt
½	cup firmly packed light brown sugar
2	cups ice cubes
2	cups apple cider or apple juice
2	cups bourbon
1	Tbsp. black peppercorns
1	(13-lb.) whole fresh turkey
	Vegetable cooking spray
¼	cup melted butter
2	Tbsp. kosher salt
1	Tbsp. onion powder
1	Tbsp. garlic powder
1	Tbsp. paprika
1	Tbsp. chopped fresh sage
1	Tbsp. chopped fresh thyme
1½	tsp. freshly ground pepper
1	Tbsp. olive oil
½	cup chopped onion
3	garlic cloves, minced
⅓	cup all-purpose flour
1	to 1½ cups chicken stock
¼	cup barbecue sauce
½	tsp. freshly ground pepper

1. Bring 6 cups water to a boil in a large stockpot over medium-high heat. Stir in 1½ cups kosher salt and brown sugar. Reduce heat, and simmer, uncovered, 2 to 3 minutes or until salt and sugar dissolve, stirring occasionally. Transfer to a large bowl; add ice and next 3 ingredients. Let stand 30 minutes or until mixture cools to room temperature, stirring occasionally.

2. Remove and discard giblets and neck from turkey. Submerge turkey in cooled brine. Cover and chill overnight.

3. Preheat oven to 325°. Coat a broiler pan and rack with cooking spray. Remove turkey from brine, discarding brine; drain well and pat dry. Tie ends of legs together with string; tuck wingtips under. Place turkey, breast side up, on rack of broiler pan. Brush turkey with melted butter. Combine 2 Tbsp. salt and next 7 ingredients in a small bowl; rub evenly over skin and inside cavity.

4. Bake, uncovered, at 325° for 2 hours and 30 minutes to 3 hours or until a meat thermometer inserted into thickest portion of thigh registers 165°. Cover loosely with aluminum foil, and let stand 25 minutes before carving.

5. Pour pan drippings from bottom of broiler pan into a glass measuring cup, and let stand 5 minutes or until fat rises to top. Spoon ¼ cup fat from top of drippings, and reserve. Discard remaining fat, reserving remaining drippings in measuring cup.

6. Heat ¼ cup reserved fat in a large saucepan over medium-high heat. Add onion and garlic; sauté 3 to 4 minutes or until tender. Sprinkle flour over onion mixture; cook, stirring constantly, 2 minutes. Add reserved turkey drippings and enough chicken stock to measure 2 cups. Bring to a boil; reduce heat, and simmer 5 minutes or until thickened. Stir in barbecue sauce and pepper. Serve with sliced turkey.

NOTE: We tested with Stubb's Original Barbecue Sauce.

SHREDDED BRUSSELS SPROUTS SALAD

MAKES 12 SERVINGS
HANDS-ON 22 MIN.   TOTAL 22 MIN.

Raw, shredded Brussels sprouts make a crisp, crunchy base for a salad. Add a few simple toppings and a homemade vinaigrette, and you have a refreshing holiday side.

12	very thin pancetta slices
¼	cup olive oil
1	Tbsp. stone-ground Dijon mustard
¼	tsp. table salt
¼	tsp. freshly ground black pepper
¼	tsp. firmly packed lemon zest
2	Tbsp. fresh lemon juice
1	garlic clove, minced
2	lb. baby Brussels sprouts, thinly sliced
½	cup chopped walnuts, toasted
2	oz. fresh Parmesan cheese, shaved

1. Cook pancetta in a large nonstick skillet over medium heat 5 minutes or until crisp, turning occasionally. Drain on paper towels.

2. Whisk together olive oil and next 6 ingredients in a large bowl. Add Brussels sprouts and walnuts; toss to coat. Divide salad among 12 plates. Top each salad with 1 pancetta crisp, and sprinkle with cheese.

SHORT RIB POT PIES *(pictured)*

MAKES 6 SERVINGS
HANDS-ON 47 MIN.   **TOTAL 3 HR., 47 MIN.**

*To save time, buy already cooked short ribs in the refrigerated
section of some warehouse stores, heat, and shred.*

2   lb. boneless beef short ribs
1¾   tsp. fine sea salt, divided
1⅛   tsp. freshly ground pepper, divided
2   Tbsp. olive oil
2   cups dry red wine
1   cup shallots, halved (3 large shallots)
3   large garlic cloves, halved
2   sprigs fresh thyme
4   cups beef stock
1½   cups sliced carrots (3 carrots)
1½   cups sliced parsnips (2 parsnips)
1   (8-oz.) package fresh cremini mushrooms, quartered
1½   (17.3-oz.) packages frozen puff pastry sheets, thawed
¼   cup all-purpose flour
¼   cup heavy cream
1   cup sour cream
2   Tbsp. prepared horseradish
Garnish: fresh thyme

1. Preheat oven to 300°. Rub ribs with 1½ tsp. salt and 1 tsp.
pepper. Cook ribs, in 2 batches, in hot oil in an oven-proof
Dutch oven over medium-high heat 2 minutes on each side
or until brown. Remove ribs from Dutch oven.

2. Add wine and next 3 ingredients to Dutch oven. Bring
to a boil; reduce heat, and simmer, uncovered, 10 minutes
or until mixture is reduced by half. Stir in stock; simmer,
uncovered, 5 minutes. Add ribs; cover and bake at 300°
for 2 hours. Turn ribs over; add carrots, parsnips, and
mushrooms; cover and bake 1 hour or until ribs are tender.
Remove from oven.

3. Increase oven temperature to 425°. Unfold pastry sheets
on a lightly floured surface. Cut each pastry sheet into
4 circles, using a 4-inch cutter. Place on an ungreased
baking sheet. Bake at 425° for 18 minutes or until golden
brown and puffed. Remove centers from circles. Keep warm.

4. Remove ribs from cooking liquid, reserving cooking
liquid. Place meat in a large bowl; separate into chunks with
2 forks.

5. Pour cooking liquid through a fine wire-mesh strainer
into a bowl. Discard thyme, reserving vegetable mixture.
Bring 2 cups strained liquid to a boil in a medium saucepan, reserving remaining liquid for another use. Combine
flour and heavy cream in a small bowl, whisking until
smooth. Whisk flour mixture into broth. Cook, whisking
constantly, until thickened and smooth. Stir in reserved
vegetables and rib meat. Cook 2 minutes or until
thoroughly heated, whisking occasionally.

6. Combine sour cream, horseradish, remaining ¼ tsp.
salt, and remaining ⅛ tsp. pepper.

7. Place pastry shells on a serving platter. Spoon meat
mixture evenly into shells. Top each with a dollop of
sour cream mixture, and garnish with fresh thyme,
if desired. Serve immediately.

CARAMELIZED ONION-
SAUSAGE CRACKER
STUFFING

MAKES 6 TO 8 SERVINGS
HANDS-ON 37 MIN.   **TOTAL 1 HR., 42 MIN.**

*Unlike traditional stuffing or dressing, this recipe uses store-
bought crackers as its base to ensure a crisp, crunchy crust.*

Vegetable cooking spray
1½   (1-lb.) packages whole wheat round buttery crackers,
      coarsely crushed
1   lb. ground pork sausage
2   Tbsp. olive oil
8   cups vertically sliced sweet onions (about 5 onions)
1   tsp. sugar
1   cup chopped celery (about 4 ribs)
2   tsp. chopped fresh sage
½   tsp. table salt
½   tsp. pepper
5   garlic cloves, minced
2   large eggs
1½   cups chicken broth
6   Tbsp. butter, melted

1. Preheat oven to 350°. Lightly grease a 13- x 9-inch
baking dish with cooking spray. Place crushed crackers in
a large bowl.

2. Cook sausage in a large skillet over medium-high heat,
stirring often, 7 minutes or until meat crumbles and is no
longer pink. Remove sausage from skillet using a slotted
spoon, and add to crushed crackers. Pour off drippings,
reserving 1 Tbsp. drippings in skillet.

3. Add olive oil to drippings in skillet. Add onions and
sugar; reduce heat to medium, and cook, stirring often,
20 minutes or until onions are caramel colored and
very tender. Stir in celery and next 4 ingredients; sauté
3 minutes or just until tender. Stir onion mixture into
sausage mixture.

4. Whisk eggs in a bowl; whisk in chicken broth. Pour broth
mixture over cracker mixture, stirring until moistened.
Spoon mixture into prepared baking dish; drizzle with
melted butter.

5. Bake, uncovered, at 350° for 55 minutes or until
browned and crisp. Let stand 10 minutes before serving.

BROWN RICE-QUINOA PILAF WITH WALNUTS, APRICOTS, AND CURRANTS

MAKES 8 SERVINGS   HANDS-ON 14 MIN.   TOTAL 14 MIN.

This simple yet flavorful side dish uses prepared rice to save you time in the kitchen over the holiday.

¼	cup chopped fresh parsley
3	Tbsp. lemon juice
½	tsp. table salt
½	tsp. freshly ground black pepper
5	Tbsp. olive oil, divided
I	large shallot, minced
I	garlic clove, minced
¾	cup chopped walnuts, toasted
¾	cup chopped dried apricots
⅓	cup currants
4	(8.5-oz.) packages ready-to-heat quinoa-and-brown rice pilaf with garlic

1. Combine first 4 ingredients and 3 Tbsp. olive oil.

2. Sauté shallot and garlic in remaining 2 Tbsp. olive oil in a large skillet over medium-high heat 3 minutes or until tender and beginning to brown. Stir in walnuts, next 3 ingredients, and lemon juice mixture. Cook, stirring constantly, 2 minutes or until thoroughly heated.

NOTE: We tested with Seeds of Change Quinoa & Brown Rice.

ROASTED ASPARAGUS WITH HOT BACON DRESSING

MAKES 10 SERVINGS   HANDS-ON 5 MIN.   TOTAL 30 MIN.

This dressing has the perfect balance of smoky, sweet, and salty flavors.

3	lb. fresh asparagus
2	Tbsp. olive oil
I	tsp. table salt, divided
¾	tsp. freshly ground black pepper, divided
8	hickory-smoked bacon slices
I	shallot, minced
2	large garlic cloves, minced
⅓	cup white wine vinegar
2	Tbsp. honey
I	tsp. Dijon mustard

1. Preheat oven to 450°. Snap off and discard tough ends of asparagus. Place asparagus on a large baking sheet. Drizzle with oil; sprinkle with ¾ tsp. salt and ½ tsp. pepper, tossing to coat.

2. Bake at 450° for 20 to 25 minutes or just until crisp-tender. Place asparagus on a serving platter; keep warm.

3. Cook bacon in a large skillet over medium-high heat until crisp; remove bacon, reserving ¼ cup drippings in skillet. Crumble bacon and set aside.

4. Sauté shallot and garlic in hot drippings 2 minutes or just until tender. Whisk in vinegar, honey, mustard, remaining ¼ tsp. salt, and remaining ¼ tsp. pepper. Cook 1 minute or until thoroughly heated. Remove from heat; stir in crumbled bacon. Drizzle hot dressing over asparagus. Serve immediately.

ROOT VEGETABLE GRATIN

MAKES 8 TO 10 SERVINGS
HANDS-ON 27 MIN.   TOTAL 1 HR., 52 MIN.

Use a mandolin to cut vegetables into thin, uniform slices.

3	cups heavy cream
6	garlic cloves, smashed
	Vegetable cooking spray
I	lb. carrots, peeled and diagonally sliced
4	tsp. chopped fresh thyme, divided
I	tsp. table salt, divided
I	tsp. freshly ground black pepper, divided
6	oz. Gruyère cheese, shredded and divided
I	lb. parsnips, peeled and diagonally sliced
¾	lb. turnips, peeled and thinly sliced
¾	lb. rutabaga, peeled and thinly sliced
I	cup panko (Japanese breadcrumbs)
2	Tbsp. butter, melted

1. Preheat oven to 400°. Combine cream and garlic in a large saucepan. Cook, stirring often, over medium heat 5 to 6 minutes or just until mixture begins to simmer (do not boil); remove from heat. Let stand 15 minutes. Remove and discard garlic. Cover and keep warm.

2. Lightly grease a 13- x 9-inch baking dish with cooking spray. Arrange carrot slices in an even layer on bottom of baking dish. Sprinkle with ¾ tsp. thyme, ¼ tsp. salt, ¼ tsp. pepper, and ⅓ cup cheese. Repeat layers 3 times, 1 time with each remaining vegetable, ¾ tsp. thyme, ¼ tsp. salt, and ¼ tsp. pepper. (Sprinkle ⅓ cup cheese over each of the first 2 repeated layers. Do not sprinkle cheese on the third repeated layer.) Pour cream over vegetables.

3. Cover and bake at 400° for 30 minutes or until vegetables are almost tender. Gently press down top layer using a metal spatula. Bake, uncovered, for 35 more minutes or until cream is reduced and thickened.

4. Combine panko, butter, remaining ½ cup cheese, and remaining 1 tsp. thyme; sprinkle over top of casserole. Bake, uncovered, 10 more minutes or until top is golden brown. Let stand 10 minutes before serving.

Root Vegetable Gratin

Brown Rice-Quinoa Pilaf with Walnuts, Apricots, and Currants

Roasted Asparagus with Hot Bacon Dressing

BRAISED BRISKET WITH RED WINE REDUCTION *(pictured)*

MAKES 6 SERVINGS
HANDS-ON 1 HR., 9 MIN.   TOTAL 4 HR., 59 MIN.

During the chaos of the holiday season, this simple braised brisket is the perfect dish, as it can be made ahead and will become even more flavorful the longer it stands. If desired, return brisket slices and finished reduction to Dutch oven or 3-quart glass dish; cover and chill until ready to reheat and serve.

1	Tbsp. kosher salt
2	tsp. freshly ground black pepper
2	tsp. granulated garlic
1	(3¼-lb.) beef brisket, trimmed
1	(750-ml.) bottle Cabernet Sauvignon or other dry red wine
1	medium leek
2	Tbsp. canola oil, divided
1	large carrot, cut into 1-inch pieces
1	large celery rib, cut into 1-inch pieces
2	shallots, sliced
5	garlic cloves, crushed
4	flat-leaf parsley sprigs
7	fresh thyme sprigs
3	bay leaves
1	qt. low-sodium beef stock
¼	cup butter, softened
¼	cup all-purpose flour

Garnish: fresh thyme leaves

1. Preheat oven to 300°. Combine first 3 ingredients. Rub both sides of brisket with salt mixture.

2. Bring red wine to a boil over medium-high heat in a medium saucepan; cook, uncovered, 14 minutes or until reduced to 1⅔ cups.

3. Meanwhile, remove and discard root end and dark green top of leek. Cut in half lengthwise, and rinse thoroughly under cold running water to remove grit and sand. Drain. Cut into 1-inch pieces.

4. Cook brisket in 1 Tbsp. hot oil in an ovenproof Dutch oven over medium-high heat 4 minutes on each side or until well browned. Remove brisket from Dutch oven. Heat remaining 1 Tbsp. oil in Dutch oven. Add leek, carrot, and next 6 ingredients; sauté 3 minutes or until lightly browned. Add reduced red wine and beef stock, stirring to loosen browned bits from bottom of Dutch oven. Return brisket to Dutch oven.

5. Cover and bake at 300° for 3½ hours or until tender, turning halfway through.

6. Transfer brisket to a platter, reserving cooking liquid in Dutch oven; cover and keep warm. Let cooking liquid stand 20 minutes. Skim and discard fat from cooking liquid; bring to a simmer in Dutch oven over medium-high heat. Simmer, uncovered, 28 minutes or until reduced to 5 cups. Pour liquid through a fine wire-mesh strainer into a bowl, pressing with the back of a wooden spoon to release liquid. Discard solids.

7. Return liquid to Dutch oven; bring to a boil. Stir together butter and flour in a small bowl until a paste forms. Whisk butter mixture into boiling liquid, whisking until smooth. Reduce heat, and simmer 5 minutes or until thickened. Cut brisket across the grain into thin slices using a sharp knife. Serve with red wine sauce. Garnish, if desired.

HERBED POTATO PANCAKES WITH CHIVE CRÈME FRAÎCHE

MAKES 14 SERVINGS
HANDS-ON 25 MIN.   TOTAL 25 MIN.

These delicious potato cakes are perfect alongside a standing rib roast or pork roast for your holiday table.

2½	lb. russet potatoes, peeled
¼	cup all-purpose flour
¼	cup chopped green onions
¼	cup chopped fresh parsley
½	tsp. table salt
2	large eggs, lightly beaten
¾	tsp. freshly ground black pepper, divided
½	cup canola oil
1	(8-oz.) container crème fraîche
½	tsp. firmly packed lemon zest
1	Tbsp. chopped fresh chives

1. Preheat oven to 200°. Line a large baking sheet with aluminum foil.

2. Peel and shred potatoes. Place potatoes, in batches, in a clean dish towel. Holding towel over a medium bowl, squeeze potatoes dry, and place in a large bowl to measure 7 cups, reserving liquid and white potato starch in medium bowl. Slowly pour off and discard liquid, reserving white potato starch in bottom of medium bowl to measure about 1½ Tbsp. Add potato starch to potatoes; stir in flour, next 4 ingredients, and ½ tsp. pepper.

3. Heat 2 Tbsp. oil in a 12-inch skillet over medium-high heat. Shape potato mixture by about ¼ cupfuls into 28 (¼-inch-thick) cakes. Fry 4 cakes in hot oil 2 to 3 minutes on each side or until edges are crisp and brown; drain on paper towels. Transfer cakes to prepared baking sheet, and keep warm in 200° oven. Repeat procedure 6 times with remaining oil and potato cakes.

4. Stir together crème fraîche, next 2 ingredients, and remaining ¼ tsp. pepper in a small bowl. Serve with potato cakes.

ROASTED VEGETABLE AND CHICKPEA STRUDELS

MAKES 12 SERVINGS
HANDS-ON 28 MIN.   TOTAL 1 HR., 38 MIN.

Strudels are often sweet, but this savory version with roasted winter vegetables, fresh thyme, and salty shredded cheese all rolled into a crisp pastry dough is the ideal option for vegetarian guests.

Vegetable cooking spray
3   cups cubed peeled butternut squash
3   cups cauliflower florets
5   carrots, peeled and cut into 1-inch pieces
4   parsnips, peeled and cut into 1-inch pieces
2   Tbsp. olive oil
2   (16-oz.) cans chickpeas, drained and rinsed
6   oz. Parmigiano-Reggiano cheese, grated
1   Tbsp. chopped fresh thyme
1   tsp. table salt
½   tsp. freshly ground black pepper
4   garlic cloves, minced
2   large eggs, lightly beaten
24   frozen phyllo sheets, thawed
⅔   cup butter, melted
Parchment paper
2   Tbsp. sesame seeds

1. Preheat oven to 450°. Coat a 15- x 10- x 1-inch jelly-roll pan with cooking spray.

2. Place squash and next 3 ingredients in a large bowl; drizzle with olive oil, tossing to coat. Spread vegetables in a single layer in prepared pan.

3. Bake at 450° for 40 minutes or until vegetables are tender and brown. Transfer vegetables to a large bowl; cool 5 minutes. Add chickpeas and next 6 ingredients, tossing to coat.

4. Reduce oven temperature to 425°.

5. Place phyllo on a flat work surface. Stack 4 phyllo sheets, brushing with melted butter between sheets (keep remaining phyllo covered with a damp towel to prevent drying out). Spoon vegetable mixture evenly down 1 long side of phyllo to within 2 inches of edge. Roll phyllo dough over filling jelly-roll style, starting with long side and tucking in edges; place on a parchment paper-lined baking sheet. Repeat procedure with remaining phyllo sheets, butter, and vegetable mixture to make 6 strudels. Brush tops of strudels with butter; sprinkle with sesame seeds.

6. Bake at 425° for 25 minutes or until phyllo is golden brown and crisp.

SEARED SCALLOPS WITH LEMON-PARMESAN DRIZZLE

(pictured)

MAKES 8 SERVINGS
HANDS-ON 15 MIN.   TOTAL 23 MIN.

Scallops may not be your idea of a traditional holiday dinner, but that's the idea behind these seared scallops. If you're looking for a seafood option that is simple, easy, and delicious, this is the holiday dish for you.

2½   lb. sea scallops (45 scallops)
½   tsp. kosher salt
¼   tsp. freshly ground black pepper
2   Tbsp. olive oil
½   cup dry white wine
½   tsp. firmly packed lemon zest
1   tsp. lemon juice
1   small shallot, minced
1   garlic clove, minced
½   cup cold butter, cut up
1   oz. Parmesan cheese, grated
1   Tbsp. whipping cream
Garnishes: lemon wedges, chopped fresh parsley

1. Rinse scallops, and pat dry with paper towels; sprinkle with salt and pepper.

2. Heat olive oil in a large skillet over medium-high heat; add one-third of scallops, and cook 3 minutes or until golden brown. Turn over; cook 1 minute. Remove from skillet; cover loosely with aluminum foil, and keep warm. Repeat procedure twice with remaining scallops.

3. Bring wine and next 4 ingredients to a boil in a small saucepan over medium-high heat. Reduce heat, and simmer, uncovered, 8 minutes or until liquid almost evaporates. Add butter, 1 piece at a time, whisking until melted and smooth after each addition. Remove from heat; whisk in cheese and cream.

4. Arrange scallops on a large serving platter. Drizzle with sauce; garnish, if desired. Serve immediately.

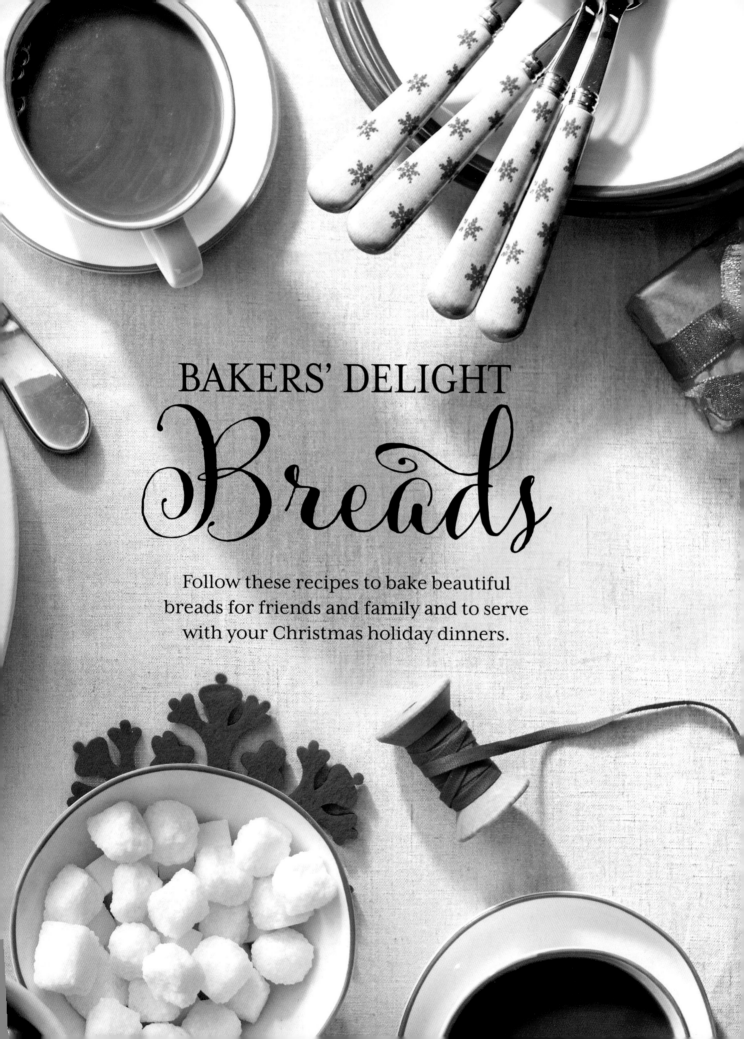

BAKERS' DELIGHT
Breads

Follow these recipes to bake beautiful
breads for friends and family and to serve
with your Christmas holiday dinners.

ORANGE-GLAZED MONKEY BREAD

MAKES 10 TO 12 SERVINGS   HANDS-ON 8 MIN.   TOTAL 53 MIN.

Try this monkey bread with a twist for a holiday dessert or even breakfast. Reserve some of the orange glaze to serve with the bread for dipping.

- 3   Tbsp. butter, softened
- ½   cup chopped pecans, toasted
- 2   (16.3-oz.) cans refrigerated jumbo
       buttermilk biscuits
- 1   cup granulated sugar
- 2½   tsp. firmly packed orange zest, divided
- ½   cup firmly packed light brown sugar
- ½   cup butter, melted
- 4   oz. cream cheese, softened
- ½   cup powdered sugar
- 3   Tbsp. fresh orange juice

1. Preheat oven to 350°. Grease a 12-cup Bundt pan with 3 Tbsp. softened butter. Sprinkle pecans in bottom of prepared Bundt pan.

2. Separate biscuits, and cut each into quarters. Combine granulated sugar and 2 tsp. orange zest in a large zip-top plastic freezer bag. Add biscuit pieces to bag; seal bag, and shake to coat. Arrange coated biscuit pieces in pan, discarding remaining sugar mixture in bag.

3. Stir together brown sugar and ½ cup melted butter. Pour over dough.

4. Bake at 350° for 40 minutes or until top is golden brown. Cool bread in pan 5 minutes; invert onto a platter.

5. Place cream cheese in a medium bowl; beat at medium speed with an electric mixer until creamy. Gradually add powdered sugar, orange juice, and remaining ½ tsp. zest, beating at low speed until blended. Drizzle orange glaze over warm bread. Serve warm.

RASPBERRY-CRANBERRY SWEET BREAD WREATH

(pictured on page 128)

MAKES 12 TO 14 SERVINGS
HANDS-ON 35 MIN.   TOTAL 4 HR., 45 MIN.

Frozen raspberries and cranberries are cooked down to make a sweet and tart jam filling for this festive braided bread.

1	cup milk (100° to 110°)
2	tsp. granulated sugar
1	(¼-oz.) envelope active dry yeast
½	cup butter, softened
½	cup granulated sugar
1	tsp. table salt
2	large eggs
1	Tbsp. firmly packed orange zest
4½	cups all-purpose flour
1½	cups frozen raspberries
1	cup frozen cranberries
⅔	cup granulated sugar
3	Tbsp. fresh orange juice
	Parchment paper
1	Tbsp. milk
1	Tbsp. coarse sugar

1. Combine first 3 ingredients in a 1-cup glass measuring cup; let stand 5 minutes.

2. Combine butter, ½ cup granulated sugar, and salt in bowl of a heavy-duty electric stand mixer. Beat at medium speed, using paddle attachment, until light and fluffy. Add eggs and orange zest, beating until blended. Beat in yeast mixture. Gradually add flour to butter mixture, beating at low speed until a soft dough forms.

3. Attach dough hook to mixer. Beat at medium-low speed 15 minutes or until dough is smooth and elastic but still soft and slightly sticky. Place in a well-greased bowl, turning to grease top.

4. Cover dough with plastic wrap, and let rise in a warm (85°) place, free from drafts, 2 hours or until doubled in bulk.

5. Meanwhile, bring raspberries and next 3 ingredients to a boil in a 3-qt. saucepan over medium-high heat, stirring often. Reduce heat to medium-low, and simmer 7 to 8 minutes or until thickened and cranberries burst, stirring occasionally. Remove from heat; cool completely (about 30 minutes). Cover and chill 1 hour or until cold.

6. Punch dough down; turn out onto a lightly floured surface. Roll dough into an 18- x 14-inch rectangle. Spread raspberry mixture over dough, leaving a 1-inch border.

7. Roll up dough, jelly-roll fashion, starting at 1 long side. Pinch seam to seal. With dough seam side down, cut roll in half lengthwise. Loosely twist roll halves around each other, keeping cut sides up. Carefully transfer to a large baking sheet lined with parchment paper; shape into a ring, pinching ends together to seal. Brush ring with 1 Tbsp. milk, and sprinkle with coarse sugar. Cover ring loosely with plastic wrap, and let rise in a warm place (85°), free from drafts, 30 minutes (dough will not double in bulk).

8. Preheat oven to 350°. Bake at 350° for 40 minutes or until ring is deep golden brown. Run wide spatulas under wreath to loosen; transfer to a wire rack, and cool completely (about 1 hour).

BACON-JALAPEÑO BUTTERMILK SCONES

MAKES 8 SERVINGS   HANDS-ON 10 MIN.   TOTAL 28 MIN.

These savory buttermilk scones spiked with bacon and jalapeño chiles make a great accompaniment for breakfast, as well as a tasty midafternoon snack.

Parchment paper

2	cups all-purpose flour
2	tsp. baking powder
½	tsp. baking soda
½	tsp. table salt
½	cup cold butter, cut up
⅓	cup pickled sliced jalapeño peppers, drained and minced
2	Tbsp. minced fresh chives
8	hickory-smoked bacon slices, cooked and crumbled
3	oz. pepper Jack cheese, shredded
¾	cup buttermilk
1	large egg, lightly beaten
1½	Tbsp. buttermilk
¼	tsp. kosher salt (optional)

1. Preheat oven to 425°. Line a baking sheet with parchment paper. Combine flour and next 3 ingredients in a large bowl. Cut butter into flour mixture with a pastry blender or fork until crumbly. Stir in pickled jalapeño peppers and next 3 ingredients. Whisk together ¾ cup buttermilk and egg. Add to flour mixture, stirring just until dry ingredients are moistened and a dough forms.

2. Turn dough out onto prepared baking sheet. Shape dough into an 8-inch circle. Cut dough into 8 wedges with a floured knife. (Do not separate wedges.)

3. Brush dough with 1½ Tbsp. buttermilk. Sprinkle with kosher salt, if desired.

4. Bake at 425° for 16 to 18 minutes or until golden brown and a wooden pick inserted in center comes out clean. Separate into wedges. Serve immediately or at room temperature.

CHEESY PIMIENTO CORNBREAD

MAKES 8 TO 10 SERVINGS
HANDS-ON 5 MIN.   TOTAL 30 MIN.

Two iconic Southern staples come together in this savory cornbread.

¼	cup butter
1¼	cups stone-ground yellow cornmeal
¾	cup all-purpose flour
1	tsp. baking soda
1	tsp. baking powder
1	tsp. table salt
¼	tsp. freshly ground black pepper
4	oz. extra-sharp Cheddar cheese, shredded
1¼	cups buttermilk
2	large eggs
1	(4-oz.) jar diced pimientos, well drained

1. Preheat oven to 425°. Place butter in a 9-inch cast-iron skillet. Place skillet in oven, and heat at 425° for 4 minutes or until butter melts. Remove skillet from oven.

2. Meanwhile, combine cornmeal and next 6 ingredients in a large bowl. Whisk together buttermilk, eggs, and pimientos; add to dry ingredients, stirring just until moistened. Pour batter over melted butter in hot skillet.

3. Bake at 425° for 25 minutes or until golden brown and a wooden pick inserted in center comes out clean.

SWEET POTATO BISCUITS WITH ROSEMARY-PECAN BUTTER

MAKES 14 SERVINGS
HANDS-ON 10 MIN.   TOTAL 30 MIN.

Sandwich leftover ham or turkey slices between halves of these biscuits for a delightful sweet-and-savory contrast.

Parchment paper
2½   cups all-purpose flour
2   Tbsp. sugar
2½   tsp. baking powder
1   tsp. ground cinnamon
½   tsp. table salt
¼   tsp. baking soda
½   cup cold butter, cut up
1   cup buttermilk
¾   cup mashed cooked sweet potato
1   Tbsp. butter, melted
Rosemary-Pecan Butter

1. Preheat oven to 450°. Line a baking sheet with parchment paper. Combine flour and next 5 ingredients in a large bowl. Cut ½ cup cold butter into flour mixture with a pastry blender or fork until mixture resembles small peas. Combine buttermilk and sweet potato; add to flour mixture, stirring just until dry ingredients are moistened.
2. Turn dough out onto a lightly floured surface, and knead lightly 3 or 4 times. Pat dough to 1-inch thickness; cut with a 2¼-inch round cutter. Place biscuits, 1 inch apart, on prepared baking sheet. Brush with melted butter.
3. Bake at 450° for 16 to 18 minutes or until light golden brown. Serve with Rosemary-Pecan Butter.

ROSEMARY-PECAN BUTTER

MAKES ¾ CUP   HANDS-ON 2 MIN.   TOTAL 2 MIN.

½   cup butter, softened
⅓   cup finely chopped pecans, toasted
1   Tbsp. honey
1   tsp. chopped fresh rosemary

Stir together all ingredients in a small bowl. Cover and store in refrigerator until ready to use. Let butter come to room temperature before using.

FEATHERLIGHT DINNER ROLLS *(pictured)*

MAKES 1 DOZEN
HANDS-ON 17 MIN.   TOTAL 2 HR., 17 MIN.

Try your hand at homemade rolls this year instead of purchasing those in the freezer section. A heavy-duty stand mixer makes quick work of these delicate rolls.

1   cup warm milk (100° to 110°)
1   (¼-oz.) envelope active dry yeast
1   tsp. sugar
3   cups all-purpose flour
2   Tbsp. sugar
1   tsp. table salt
5   Tbsp. melted butter, divided
1   large egg, lightly beaten
Vegetable cooking spray

1. Stir together first 3 ingredients in a 2-cup glass measuring cup; let stand 5 minutes.
2. Combine flour and next 2 ingredients in bowl of a heavy-duty electric stand mixer. Add 3 Tbsp. melted butter, egg, and yeast mixture; beat at low speed, using dough hook attachment, 3 minutes or until blended and a soft dough forms. Increase speed to medium-low, and beat 4 minutes or until dough is smooth and elastic but still slightly sticky. Cover bowl of dough with plastic wrap, and let rise in a warm (85°) place, free from drafts, 1 hour or until doubled in bulk.
3. Lightly grease a 13- x 9-inch pan with cooking spray. Punch dough down. Turn dough out onto a lightly floured surface. Divide dough into 12 equal portions. Gently shape each portion into a 2-inch ball; place in prepared pan. Brush tops with 1 Tbsp. melted butter. Cover and let rise in a warm (85°) place, free from drafts, 45 minutes or until doubled in bulk.
4. Preheat oven to 375°. Bake rolls at 375° for 15 minutes or until golden brown. Transfer rolls from pan to a wire rack, and brush with remaining 1 Tbsp. melted butter. Serve warm, or cool completely (about 30 minutes).

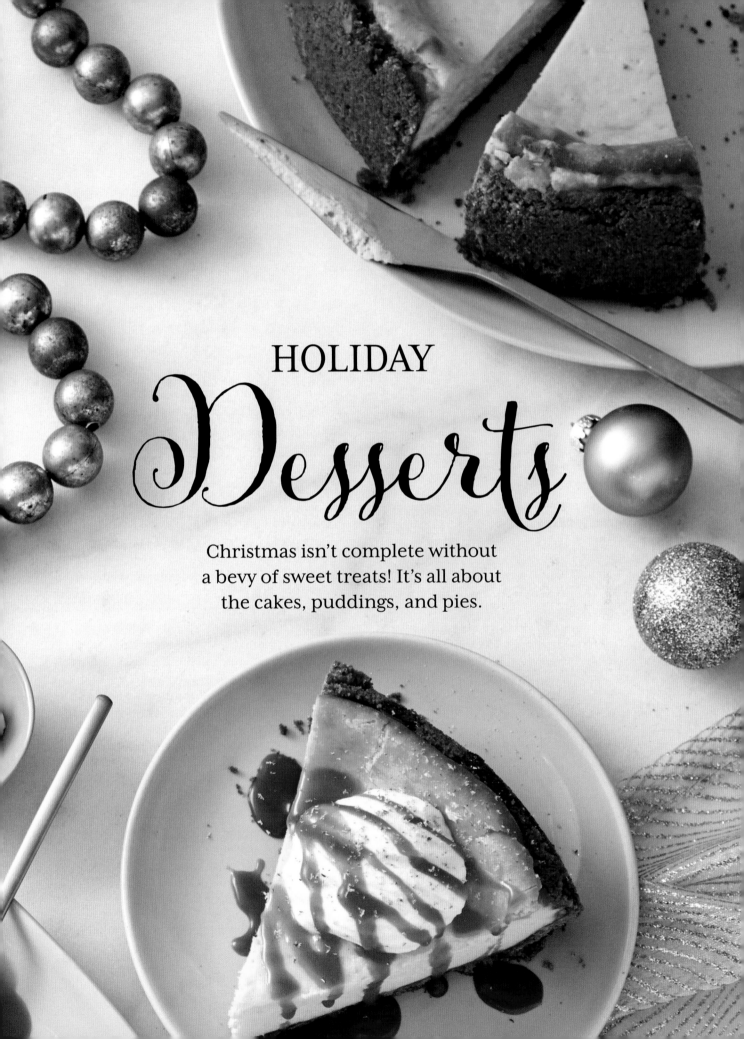

HOLIDAY

Desserts

Christmas isn't complete without
a bevy of sweet treats! It's all about
the cakes, puddings, and pies.

EGGNOG CHEESECAKE WITH BOURBON CARAMEL

(pictured on page 136)

MAKES 10 SERVINGS   HANDS-ON 15 MIN.
TOTAL 11 HR., 36 MIN., INCLUDING CHILL TIME

You can also use high-quality prepared caramel sauce. Warm it in a saucepan over low heat, then gradually stir in bourbon to taste.

2   cups graham cracker crumbs (about 15 whole crackers)
½   cup butter, melted
½   cup finely chopped pecans
2   Tbsp. sugar
3   (8-oz.) packages cream cheese, softened
1¾   cups sugar, divided
2   Tbsp. all-purpose flour
½   tsp. freshly grated nutmeg
4   large eggs
1   cup refrigerated eggnog
1   tsp. vanilla extract
¼   cup light corn syrup
¾   cup heavy whipping cream
2   Tbsp. bourbon
Sweetened whipped cream
Freshly grated nutmeg

1. Preheat oven to 325°. Stir together first 4 ingredients in a medium bowl until well blended. Press mixture on bottom and 2 inches up sides of a 9-inch springform pan. Bake for 10 to 12 minutes or until lightly browned. Remove crust to a wire rack, and cool completely (about 30 minutes).

2. Meanwhile, beat cream cheese and 1 cup sugar at medium speed with a heavy-duty electric stand mixer until blended and smooth. Beat in flour and nutmeg. Add eggs, 1 at a time, beating just until blended after each addition. Add eggnog and vanilla, beating until blended. Pour batter into prepared crust.

3. Bake at 325° for 1 hour and 5 minutes or until almost set. Turn oven off. Let cheesecake stand in oven with door closed 15 minutes. Remove cheesecake from oven, and gently run a knife around outer edge of cheesecake to loosen from sides of pan. (Do not remove sides of pan.) Cool completely on a wire rack (about 1 hour). Cover and chill 8 to 24 hours.

4. Bring corn syrup, ¼ cup water, and remaining ¾ cup sugar to a boil in a medium saucepan over medium-high heat. (Do not stir.) Boil, swirling occasionally after sugar begins to change color, 7 minutes or until dark amber. (Do not walk away from the pan because sugar will burn quickly once it begins to change color.) Remove from heat. Carefully whisk in cream (mixture will bubble and spatter). Whisk constantly until bubbling stops and caramel dissolves. Whisk in bourbon. Cover and refrigerate until ready to use or up to 2 weeks.

5. Remove sides of pan from cheesecake. Insert a medium-size metal star tip into a large decorating bag; fill with whipped cream. Pipe cream decoratively around top edge of cheesecake. Sprinkle with freshly grated nutmeg. Heat caramel until pourable. Drizzle each serving with caramel.

RASPBERRY SWIRL ICEBOX PIE *(pictured)*

MAKES 8 TO 10 SERVINGS
HANDS-ON 22 MIN.   TOTAL 7 HR., 8 MIN.

This colorful make-ahead raspberry mousse pie in pistachio shortbread crust is perfect for no-fuss holiday entertaining.

½   cup pistachios
13   rectangular pure butter shortbread cookies, broken
¼   cup butter, melted
Vegetable cooking spray
½   cup sugar
1   envelope unflavored gelatin
1   Tbsp. fresh lemon juice
4   cups frozen raspberries, thawed
1   cup heavy cream
Garnishes: whipped cream, fresh raspberries, lemon zest, and fresh mint sprigs

1. Preheat oven to 350°. Process pistachios in a food processor until chopped. Add cookies, and process until finely ground. Add butter; pulse just until crumbs are moistened. Press crumb mixture into bottom and up sides of a 9½-inch deep-dish pie plate coated with cooking spray.

2. Bake at 350° for 16 minutes or until golden brown. Cool completely on a wire rack (about 30 minutes).

3. Bring sugar and ¼ cup water to a simmer in a small saucepan, stirring until sugar dissolves. Remove from heat.

4. Sprinkle gelatin over 2 Tbsp. cold water in a small bowl; let stand 1 minute. Add gelatin mixture to warm sugar mixture, stirring until gelatin dissolves (about 2 minutes). Transfer to a large bowl; stir in lemon juice.

5. Process raspberries in clean food processor until smooth. Pour raspberry purée through a wire-mesh strainer into a bowl, pressing with the back of a spoon to squeeze out juice. Discard pulp and seeds. Whisk 1 cup raspberry purée into gelatin mixture, reserving remaining purée for later use.

6. Beat cream at medium speed with an electric mixer until soft peaks form. Whisk one-fourth of whipped cream into gelatin mixture; fold in remaining whipped cream. Spoon mixture into prepared crust. Dollop remaining raspberry purée, by teaspoonfuls, onto top of pie; gently swirl into filling with a knife. Cover and refrigerate at least 6 hours or up to overnight. Garnish, if desired.

NOTE: We tested with Walker's Pure Butter Shortbread.

CHOCOLATE-BANANA PUDDING

MAKES 8 TO 10 SERVINGS
HANDS-ON 30 MIN.   TOTAL 4 HR., 30 MIN.

Be sure to use soft ladyfingers found in the bakery department of your grocery store.

I	envelope unflavored gelatin
¾	cup granulated sugar
⅓	cup unsweetened cocoa
5	large egg yolks
3½	cups heavy cream, divided
I	tsp. vanilla extract
I	cup semisweet mini-morsels, divided
1½	(3-oz.) packages ladyfingers
¼	cup coffee liqueur
¼	cup brewed coffee
4	medium bananas, sliced

Garnish: chocolate curls

1. Sprinkle gelatin over ¼ cup cold water in a small bowl.

2. Whisk together sugar and cocoa in a large saucepan until blended. Whisk in egg yolks and 2 cups cream. Cook, whisking constantly, over medium heat 5 to 6 minutes or until thickened. Remove from heat; stir in gelatin mixture and vanilla, whisking until gelatin dissolves.

3. Fill a large bowl with ice. Place pan containing custard in ice, and let stand 10 minutes or until custard cools to room temperature, stirring occasionally.

4. Meanwhile, place ½ cup mini-morsels in a small microwave-safe bowl; microwave at HIGH 30 to 60 seconds, stirring every 30 seconds until smooth.

5. Beat remaining 1½ cups heavy cream at high speed with an electric mixer until soft peaks form. Add melted chocolate and remaining ½ cup mini-morsels to custard, stirring until blended. Gently fold in 2 cups whipped cream. Cover and chill remaining whipped cream.

6. Layer half of ladyfingers in an 8-inch square baking dish. Combine liqueur and coffee. Brush half of coffee mixture over ladyfingers in dish. Top with half of banana slices and half of custard. Repeat procedure with remaining ladyfingers, coffee mixture, banana slices, and custard. Cover and chill 4 hours or until set.

7. Spread remaining 1 cup whipped cream over custard just before serving. Garnish, if desired.

NOTE: We tested with Kahlúa.

SPICED PRALINE APPLE CAKE

MAKES 12 SERVINGS   HANDS-ON 28 MIN.   TOTAL 4 HR., 6 MIN.

Ground toasted pecans and chopped apples give this moist, delicately spiced Bundt cake a comforting appeal. Serve without the rich praline frosting as a snack or coffee cake.

CAKE
Shortening
1	cup pecans, toasted and cooled
2½	cups all-purpose flour
2	tsp. apple pie spice
1	tsp. baking powder
½	tsp. baking soda
½	tsp. table salt
1	cup butter, softened
2	cups firmly packed light brown sugar
4	large eggs
1	tsp. vanilla extract
1	(8-oz.) container sour cream
2½	cups finely chopped peeled Fuji apples

PRALINE GLAZE
½	cup firmly packed light brown sugar
¼	cup butter
¼	cup half-and-half
1	tsp. vanilla extract
1	cup powdered sugar

Garnishes: dried apple chips, toasted pecan halves

1. Prepare Cake: Preheat oven to 350°. Grease (with shortening) and flour a 12-cup Bundt pan. Process pecans in a food processor until finely chopped. Whisk together pecans, 2½ cups flour, and next 4 ingredients in a bowl.

2. Beat butter at medium speed with an electric mixer until creamy. Gradually add brown sugar, beating until well blended. Add eggs, 1 at a time, beating just until blended after each addition. Beat in vanilla. Add flour mixture to butter mixture alternately with sour cream, beginning and ending with flour mixture. Beat batter at low speed just until blended after each addition. Stir in apples. Spoon batter into prepared pan.

3. Bake at 350° for 1 hour or until a long wooden pick inserted in center comes out clean. Cool cake in pan on a wire rack 15 minutes; remove from pan to wire rack, and cool completely (about 2 hours).

4. Prepare Glaze: Bring first 3 ingredients to a boil in a 2-qt. saucepan, whisking constantly; boil 1 minute. Remove from heat; stir in vanilla. Gradually whisk in powdered sugar until smooth; stir gently 5 minutes or until mixture begins to cool and thickens slightly. Spoon immediately over cooled cake. Garnish, if desired.

COCONUT-RED VELVET TRIFLE

(pictured on page 145)

MAKES 18 TO 20 SERVINGS
HANDS-ON 29 MIN.   TOTAL 2 HR., 29 MIN.

Make sure to chill the trifle before serving so the filling will have time to soak into the cake.

CAKE

3	cups all-purpose flour
2	Tbsp. unsweetened cocoa
1½	tsp. baking soda
½	tsp. table salt
1	cup butter, softened
1½	cups granulated sugar
3	large eggs
1	cup buttermilk
1	tsp. white vinegar
1	tsp. vanilla extract
1	(1-oz.) bottle red liquid food coloring
Shortening	

FILLING

2	cups heavy cream
2	(8-oz.) packages cream cheese, softened
1	cup powdered sugar
⅓	cup cream of coconut

TRIFLE

1	(7-oz.) package sweetened flaked coconut, toasted
½	cup chopped pecans, toasted

1. Prepare Cake: Preheat oven to 350°. Whisk together first 4 ingredients in a large bowl.

2. Beat butter at medium speed with an electric mixer until creamy. Gradually add granulated sugar, beating until light and fluffy. Add eggs, 1 at a time, beating just until blended after each addition. Add flour mixture to butter mixture alternately with buttermilk, beginning and ending with flour mixture. Beat at low speed until blended after each addition, stopping to scrape bowl as needed. Stir in vinegar, vanilla, and food coloring. Pour batter into 3 greased (with shortening) and floured 8-inch square cake pans.

3. Bake at 350° for 20 minutes or until wooden pick inserted in center comes out clean. Cool in pans on wire racks 10 minutes; remove from pans to wire racks, and cool completely (about 30 minutes).

4. Prepare Filling: Beat heavy cream at high speed with an electric mixer until soft peaks form. Place cream cheese in a separate bowl; beat at medium speed with an electric mixer until creamy. Gradually add powdered sugar and cream of coconut, beating until blended.

5. Gently stir one-fourth of whipped cream into cream cheese mixture using rubber spatula; fold in remaining whipped cream.

6. Assemble Trifle: Cut cake into 1-inch cubes. Layer one-third of cake cubes in a 6- to 7-qt. trifle dish. Top with one-third each of filling and coconut. Repeat layers twice. Cover and chill at least 1 hour. Sprinkle with pecans just before serving.

COCONUT-CITRUS PAVLOVA

(pictured on page 144)

MAKES 12 SERVINGS
HANDS-ON 35 MIN.   TOTAL 4 HR., 35 MIN.

Australians and New Zealanders argue as to the origin of this dessert, but one thing is clear: Its billowy meringue with a crisp exterior and luscious citrus cream topping is ethereal.

CITRUS CURD

5	large egg yolks
½	cup sugar
⅛	tsp. table salt
1	tsp. firmly packed lemon zest
1	tsp. firmly packed orange zest
¼	cup fresh lemon juice
¼	cup fresh orange juice
6	Tbsp. butter, cut into 6 pieces

MERINGUE

1¼	cups sugar
1½	Tbsp. cornstarch
5	large egg whites
¼	tsp. cream of tartar
⅛	tsp. table salt
½	tsp. vanilla extract
Parchment paper	

PAVLOVA

¾	cup whipping cream
2	cups assorted citrus sections, such as orange, blood orange, grapefruit, and tangerine
½	cup shaved fresh coconut, lightly toasted

1. Prepare Curd: Whisk together first 5 ingredients in a 2-qt. saucepan. Whisk in citrus juices. Cook, whisking constantly, over medium heat 5 minutes or until thick (do not boil). Remove from heat; add butter, 1 Tbsp. at a time, whisking until melted and curd is smooth and creamy. Pour curd through a wire-mesh strainer into a medium bowl. Place plastic wrap directly onto surface of curd (to prevent a film from forming), and chill 2 to 24 hours.

2. Prepare Meringue: Preheat oven to 225°. Whisk together sugar and cornstarch in a bowl. Beat egg whites at medium-high speed with a heavy-duty electric stand mixer 1 minute; add cream of tartar and salt, beating until blended. Gradually add sugar mixture, 1 Tbsp. at a time, beating at medium-high speed until mixture is glossy, stiff peaks form, and sugar dissolves. (Do not overbeat.) Beat in vanilla. Gently spread mixture into a 9-inch circle on a parchment paper-lined baking sheet, making a large indentation in center of meringue to hold filling.

3. Bake at 225° for 2 hours or until outside has formed a crust. Turn oven off; let meringue stand in oven, with door closed, 2 hours or until completely cool and dry.

4. Prepare Pavlova: Carefully remove meringue from parchment paper, and place on a serving platter. Beat whipping cream at high speed with an electric mixer until stiff peaks form; gently fold whipped cream into curd. Spoon curd mixture onto center of meringue; top with citrus sections and coconut. Serve immediately.

SWEET POTATO TARTLETS WITH CRÈME FRAÎCHE TOPPING

(pictured on page 144)

MAKES 6 SERVINGS
HANDS-ON 25 MIN.   **TOTAL 3 HR., 48 MIN.**

We prefer to bake fresh sweet potatoes to use in these individual tarts because it brings out their natural sweetness. Puréeing them in a food processor instead of mashing them creates a silkier texture in the filling.

1¼   lb. sweet potatoes (2 medium)
Vegetable cooking spray
1   (7.25-oz.) package shortbread cookies
⅓   cup toasted sliced almonds
1   Tbsp. granulated sugar
¼   cup butter, melted
1½   cups heavy cream, divided
⅓   cup granulated sugar
⅓   cup firmly packed dark brown sugar
1   tsp. vanilla extract
¾   tsp. ground cinnamon
½   tsp. table salt
½   tsp. ground ginger
¼   tsp. freshly grated nutmeg
2   large eggs
⅓   cup crème fraîche
2   tsp. dark brown sugar
Garnishes: toasted pecan halves, freshly grated nutmeg

1. Preheat oven to 450°. Scrub sweet potatoes; rinse and pat dry with paper towels. Coat potatoes with cooking spray, and place in a small shallow baking pan lined with aluminum foil. Bake at 450° for 1 hour or until very tender.

Remove from oven; reduce oven temperature to 350°. Cool potatoes on a wire rack (about 30 minutes); peel.

2. Meanwhile, lightly grease 6 (4½- x ¾-inch) round tartlet pans with cooking spray. Process cookies and next 2 ingredients in a food processor until finely ground. Drizzle butter over cookie mixture; pulse 5 times or until blended. Press about ⅓ cup cookie mixture in bottom and up sides of each prepared tartlet pan; place on a baking sheet.

3. Bake at 350° for 14 minutes or until golden brown. Remove from baking sheet to a wire rack, and cool completely (about 30 minutes).

4. Meanwhile, wipe processor bowl clean with a paper towel. Process sweet potatoes in food processor 20 to 30 seconds or until smooth and silky, stopping to scrape down sides as needed. Add ¾ cup cream and next 8 ingredients; process 15 to 30 seconds or just until blended and smooth, stopping to scrape down sides as needed. Pour mixture evenly into cooled tartlet shells.

5. Bake at 350° for 23 minutes or just until filling is set. Cool completely on a wire rack (about 1 hour).

6. Beat crème fraîche, 2 tsp. dark brown sugar, and remaining ¾ cup heavy cream at high speed with an electric mixer until stiff peaks form. Dollop topping over tartlets.

NOTE: We tested with Pepperidge Farm Chessmen Cookies.

holiday hints
MAKE AHEAD

Get a jump-start on your busy holiday menu preparations and make these sweet potato tartlets a day in advance. Assemble the pies and refrigerate until they're ready to serve. Just before dessert, whip up the crème fraîche topping and dollop over the tartlets.

If sweet potato casserole is on your menu, kill two birds with one stone and bake up extra sweet potatoes for the tartlets while preparing your casserole. Set the additional potatoes aside to use later in the tartlet filling.

Sweet Potato Tartlets
with Crème Fraîche
Topping

Coconut-Citrus Pavlova

Coconut–Red
Velvet Trifle

GINGERBREAD ROULADE

MAKES 8 TO 10 SERVINGS
HANDS-ON 35 MIN.   TOTAL 3 HR., 47 MIN.

This cake roll is easiest to slice when chilled, but it tastes best when eaten at room temperature. Let slices stand on serving plates for 10 to 15 minutes before serving, if desired.

CAKE
Vegetable cooking spray
Parchment paper
Shortening
⅔ cup cake flour
1½ tsp. ground cinnamon
1½ tsp. ground ginger
½ tsp. baking powder
¼ tsp. table salt
¼ tsp. ground cloves
¼ tsp. ground allspice
4 large eggs, separated
½ cup granulated sugar, divided
3 Tbsp. molasses
3 Tbsp. butter, melted
1 tsp. vanilla extract
⅓ cup powdered sugar

SYRUP
¼ cup granulated sugar
2 Tbsp. ginger liqueur or brandy

FROSTING
1 cup heavy cream
2 Tbsp. brandy
1 (8-oz.) container mascarpone cheese, softened
¼ cup powdered sugar
⅛ tsp. table salt
Chopped crystallized ginger
Garnish: white chocolate snowflakes

1. Prepare Cake: Preheat oven to 400°. Lightly grease a 15- x 10-inch jelly-roll pan with cooking spray, and line with parchment paper. Grease parchment paper (with shortening), and dust with flour.

2. Whisk together cake flour and next 6 ingredients in a medium bowl. Beat egg yolks and ¼ cup granulated sugar at high speed with electric mixer until thick and pale. Reduce speed to low. Beat in molasses, butter, and vanilla. Sift flour mixture over egg yolk mixture, in 3 additions, gently folding in flour mixture after each addition.

3. Thoroughly clean beaters. Beat egg whites at medium speed with an electric mixer until foamy; gradually add remaining ¼ cup granulated sugar, beating until stiff peaks form and sugar dissolves. Gently fold egg white mixture into batter. Gently spread batter in prepared pan.

4. Bake at 400° for 10 minutes or until a wooden pick inserted in center comes out clean and top is lightly browned.

5. Sprinkle ⅓ cup powdered sugar over top of cake. Invert cake onto a parchment paper-lined surface. Peel top layer of parchment from cake. Starting at 1 short side, immediately roll cake and bottom parchment paper together. Cool completely (about 1 hour).

6. Prepare Syrup: Combine sugar and ¼ cup water in a small saucepan over medium-high heat. Bring to a simmer, stirring until sugar dissolves. Remove from heat; cool 5 minutes. Stir in liqueur.

7. Prepare Frosting: Beat cream and brandy at high speed with an electric mixer until stiff peaks form. Stir together mascarpone, powdered sugar, and salt in a separate bowl until blended. Gently fold whipped cream mixture into mascarpone mixture until blended. Reserve 1½ cups frosting; cover and chill for later use.

8. Unroll cake onto a flat surface. Poke holes all over cake with a wooden pick. Brush syrup onto cake in several additions, letting syrup soak into cake after each addition. Spread remaining 1½ cups frosting over cake, leaving a 1-inch border on all sides. Lift and tilt parchment paper, and roll up cake in jelly-roll fashion, starting at 1 short side and using parchment paper as a guide. Place cake, wrapped in parchment paper, on a baking sheet. Chill 2 to 24 hours.

9. Transfer cake to a serving platter; remove and discard parchment paper. Top with reserved chilled frosting; sprinkle with crystallized ginger. Garnish, if desired.

FOR WHITE CHOCOLATE SNOWFLAKES: Melt 4 oz. chopped white chocolate in a small microwave-safe bowl on HIGH 1 to 1½ minutes, stirring every 30 seconds. Spoon into a piping bag fitted with a #3 plain tip. Pipe snowflake patterns onto a parchment paper-lined baking sheet. Refrigerate 30 minutes or until set. Carefully remove from parchment, and place on cake. Snowflake stencils can also be printed from the Internet.

CHOCOLATE PEPPERMINT LAYER CAKE *(pictured)*

MAKES 12 TO 16 SERVINGS
HANDS-ON 30 MIN.   TOTAL 2 HR., 15 MIN.

This decadent dessert combines the rich flavor of chocolate with a holiday staple: peppermint. It's the perfect statement for your holiday meal.

CAKE
Shortening
Parchment paper
2   cups granulated sugar
2   cups all-purpose flour
1   tsp. baking soda
½   tsp. table salt
1   cup unsalted butter
¼   cup unsweetened dark cocoa
3   oz. bittersweet chocolate, chopped
½   cup buttermilk
2   large eggs, lightly beaten
1   tsp. vanilla extract

PEPPERMINT BUTTERCREAM FROSTING
1½   cups unsalted butter, softened
8   cups powdered sugar, sifted
1   tsp. vanilla extract
½   tsp. peppermint extract
⅛   tsp. table salt
¼   cup heavy cream
½   cup crushed peppermint stick candies
2   drops red liquid food coloring
Garnishes: red and white curls, white chocolate snowflakes

1. Prepare Cake: Preheat oven to 350°. Grease (with shortening) 2 (8-inch) round cake pans. Line pans with parchment paper; grease parchment paper, and dust with flour.

2. Combine granulated sugar, flour, baking soda, and salt in a large bowl. Bring butter, cocoa, and 1 cup water to a boil in a small saucepan over medium-high heat, whisking often until butter melts. Add chocolate, whisking until melted. Whisk butter mixture into flour mixture until blended. Add buttermilk, eggs, and vanilla; whisk until blended. Pour batter into prepared pans.

3. Bake at 350° for 30 to 35 minutes or until a wooden pick inserted in center comes out clean. Cool in pans on wire racks 10 minutes. Remove from pans. Cool completely on wire racks (about 1 hour). Cut layers in half horizontally.

4. Prepare Frosting: Place butter in a large bowl; beat at medium speed with an electric mixer until creamy. Gradually add powdered sugar, beating at low speed until blended. Beat in vanilla, peppermint extract, and salt. Add cream; beat at medium speed 1 minute or until

smooth. Transfer 2¼ cups frosting to a bowl. Stir in crushed peppermint candies and red food coloring; spread ¾ cup between layers. Spread remaining 3¼ cups frosting on top and sides of cake. Garnish, if desired.

NOTE: We tested with Hershey's Special Dark Cocoa.

FOR WHITE CHOCOLATE SNOWFLAKES: Melt 4 oz. chopped white chocolate in a small microwave-safe bowl on HIGH 1 to 1½ minutes, stirring every 30 seconds. Spoon into a piping bag fitted with a #3 plain tip. Pipe snowflake patterns onto a parchment paper-lined baking sheet. Refrigerate 30 minutes or until set. Carefully remove from parchment, and place on cake. Snowflake stencils can also be printed from the Internet.

CHOCOLATE-HAZELNUT POTS DE CREME

MAKES 8 SERVINGS
HANDS-ON 22 MIN.   TOTAL 4 HR., 27 MIN.

This easy make-ahead dessert will definitely be a crowd-pleaser among chocolate lovers. Garnish with pieces of Hazelnut Brittle (page 165) for an even more impressive presentation.

1½   cups heavy cream
1   cup milk
¼   cup sugar
⅛   tsp. table salt
6   large egg yolks
6   oz. bittersweet chocolate, finely chopped
¾   cup hazelnut spread
2   Tbsp. hazelnut liqueur
Sweetened whipped cream

1. Cook first 4 ingredients in a heavy medium saucepan over medium heat, stirring often, 4 minutes or just until mixture begins to steam (do not boil); remove from heat.

2. Whisk egg yolks in a medium bowl. Gradually whisk 1 cup hot cream mixture into egg yolks; gradually whisk egg mixture into hot cream mixture.

3. Cook, stirring constantly, over medium heat 5 minutes or until slightly thickened and a thermometer registers 160°. (Do not boil.) Add chocolate, hazelnut spread, and liqueur; let stand 2 minutes. (Chocolate may look curdled at this point.) Whisk until chocolate melts. Process in a blender until smooth. Pour mixture into 8 (4-oz.) ramekins. Cover and chill at least 4 hours.

4. Top with whipped cream. Garnish with Hazelnut Brittle or toasted hazelnuts, if desired.

NOTE: We tested with Nutella and Frangelico.

TOMORROW'S
Leftovers

Give that extra turkey, ham, and roast beef
a second try as a soup, sandwich, or pizza!

BEEF TENDERLOIN AND CARAMELIZED ONION HOAGIES *(pictured)*

MAKES 4 SERVINGS
HANDS-ON 21 MIN.   **TOTAL 39 MIN.**

One of the best parts about cooking a whole beef tenderloin for the holidays is having leftover meat for sandwiches. This version takes advantage of medium-rare meat, pairing it with succulent caramelized onions on French rolls. If you have leftover horseradish sauce from the meal, use that to take your hoagies to yet another level of deliciousness.

Vegetable cooking spray
4   French sandwich rolls
1   Tbsp. butter
1   Tbsp. olive oil
6   cups sliced onion (2 large)
1   tsp. sugar
1¼ tsp. table salt, divided
1   tsp. freshly ground black pepper, divided
3   Tbsp. prepared horseradish
1   (8-oz.) container sour cream
1   lb. cooked beef tenderloin, thinly sliced
8   Provolone cheese slices
1   large tomato, sliced
2   cups arugula

1. Preheat broiler with oven rack 6 inches from heat. Line a baking sheet with aluminum foil; coat foil with cooking spray.

2. Make a lengthwise cut in 1 side of each roll, cutting to but not through the opposite side. Coat cut sides of rolls with cooking spray. Place rolls, cut sides up, on prepared baking sheet. Broil 30 seconds to 1 minute or until lightly toasted.

3. Place butter and olive oil in a large skillet; heat over medium-high heat until butter melts. Add onion, sugar, 1 tsp. salt, and ½ tsp. pepper. Cook, stirring often, 15 minutes or until onion is caramel colored.

4. Stir together horseradish, sour cream, remaining ¼ tsp. salt, and remaining ½ tsp. pepper in a bowl. Spread about 2 Tbsp. horseradish mixture on both sides of each roll. Place one-fourth of beef slices on cut side of each roll bottom; spoon ¼ cup caramelized onion on cut side of each roll top. Place 1 cheese slice on each side of rolls.

5. Broil 2 minutes or until cheese melts. Transfer rolls to plates. Top cheese on beef side of rolls evenly with tomato slices and arugula. Close sandwiches; cut in half crosswise. Serve immediately.

HEAVENLY HAM BONE SOUP

(pictured on page 150)

MAKES 10 SERVINGS
HANDS-ON 10 MIN.   **TOTAL 1 HR., 35 MIN.**

In some families, getting the leftover ham bone after a holiday meal is a gift in itself. Use this recipe to make the most of your holiday leftovers and to create a comforting, filling soup for the coldest weeks of winter.

2   celery ribs, quartered
1   (3-lb.) meaty ham bone
1   large carrot, halved
1   medium onion, halved
1   bay leaf
1   Tbsp. olive oil
1   cup diced onion
½   cup diced carrot
½   cup diced celery
4   large garlic cloves, minced
1   (14.5-oz.) can diced tomatoes, undrained
3   cups drained cooked butter beans, black-eyed peas, or pinto beans
2   cups drained cooked collard greens, turnip greens, or kale

1. Bring first 5 ingredients and 12 cups water to a boil in a large stockpot; reduce heat, and simmer, uncovered, 1 hour. Remove ham bone; cool completely. Pour broth through a sieve into a large bowl. Reserve any pieces of ham; discard remaining solids.

2. Heat olive oil in a Dutch oven over medium-high heat. Add diced onion and next 3 ingredients; cook, stirring often, 5 to 6 minutes or until vegetables are tender. Stir in tomatoes, beans, greens, reserved ham, and 8 cups reserved broth; reserve remaining broth for another use, or discard. Stir in 1 cup water. Bring to a boil; reduce heat, and simmer, uncovered, 20 minutes, stirring occasionally.

MASHED POTATO AND SAUSAGE HAND PIES

MAKES 8 SERVINGS
HANDS-ON 25 MIN.   TOTAL 1 HR.

Utilize your leftover Christmas mashed potatoes with these quick and easy hand pies. You can also swap out sausage for turkey or ham. Serve with leftover gravy as a dipping sauce.

I	lb. ground pork sausage
2	cups chopped trimmed collard greens
I	cup mashed potatoes
4	oz. cream cheese, softened
½	tsp. hot sauce
¼	tsp. table salt
¼	tsp. freshly ground black pepper
I	(17.3-oz.) package frozen puff pastry sheets, thawed
I	large egg, beaten

Parchment paper

1. Preheat oven to 400°. Brown sausage in a large skillet over medium-high heat, stirring often, 6 to 8 minutes or until sausage crumbles and is no longer pink. Remove sausage from skillet using a slotted spoon; reserve drippings in skillet.

2. Cook collard greens in drippings 3 minutes or until wilted, stirring often. Combine collard greens, cooked sausage, mashed potatoes, and next 4 ingredients.

3. Roll each puff pastry sheet into a 10-inch square on a lightly floured surface. Cut each square into 4 (5-inch) squares. Place about ½ cup potato mixture in center of each pastry square. Brush edges with egg. Fold 1 corner of each square over filling to opposite corner to make triangles, pressing edges to seal. Place on baking sheets lined with parchment paper.

4. Bake at 400° for 20 to 25 minutes or until golden and puffed. Transfer to a wire rack; cool 10 minutes. Serve warm.

CREAMY TURKEY-PECAN SLAW

MAKES 8 SERVINGS   HANDS-ON 12 MIN.
TOTAL 1 HR., 12 MIN., INCLUDING CHILL TIME

Reinvent leftover turkey in this simple slaw dish. Or, substitute deli rotisserie turkey breast or chicken if you'd like.

⅔	cup mayonnaise
2	Tbsp. apple cider vinegar
I	Tbsp. chopped fresh chives
2	tsp. Dijon mustard
½	tsp. table salt
¼	tsp. freshly ground black pepper
I	(16-oz.) package shredded coleslaw mix
2	cups shredded roasted turkey breast
I	cup chopped Granny Smith apple
½	cup sweetened dried cranberries
½	cup coarsely chopped pecans, toasted

Whisk together first 6 ingredients in a large bowl. Add coleslaw mix and next 4 ingredients, tossing to coat. Cover and chill until ready to serve.

CURRIED TURKEY AND LENTIL STEW

MAKES 6 SERVINGS
HANDS-ON 17 MIN.   TOTAL 53 MIN.

Serve this hearty stew with toasted French bread or other crusty bread.

I	cup chopped onion
I	cup chopped carrots
I	Tbsp. olive oil
2	garlic cloves, minced
2	tsp. curry powder
4	cups shredded rotisserie turkey breast or leftover turkey
6	cups chicken broth
I	(14.5-oz.) can diced tomatoes
1½	cups dried lentils
½	tsp. table salt
½	cup plain yogurt

Sauté onion and carrots in hot oil in a large Dutch oven over medium-high heat 6 minutes or until tender. Add garlic and curry powder; sauté 1 minute. Stir in turkey and next 4 ingredients. Bring to a boil; reduce heat, and simmer 35 minutes or until lentils are tender. Serve with yogurt.

HOLIDAY VEGGIE PIZZA

MAKES 4 SERVINGS
HANDS-ON 14 MIN.   TOTAL 29 MIN.

Be sure to remove any sweet toppings from your leftover
sweet potato casserole if using for this pizza.

4	hickory-smoked bacon slices
½	cup sliced onion
1	cup sliced Brussels sprouts (6 large)
1	lb. fresh pizza dough
1	cup mashed cooked sweet potato or leftover sweet potato casserole
1	cup (4 oz.) shredded Monterey Jack cheese
¼	cup chopped pecans
½	cup canned whole-berry cranberry sauce
1	tsp. minced canned chipotle pepper in adobo sauce
¼	tsp. table salt
¼	tsp. freshly ground pepper

1. Preheat oven to 475°. Cook bacon in a large skillet over medium-high heat 5 to 6 minutes or until crisp; remove bacon, and drain on paper towels, reserving drippings in skillet. Crumble bacon.

2. Sauté onion in hot drippings 2 minutes. Add Brussels sprouts; sauté 2 minutes or until vegetables are tender.

3. Roll pizza dough into a 12-inch circle. Transfer to an ungreased baking sheet. Spread mashed sweet potato over dough, leaving a 1-inch border. Top with Brussels sprouts mixture and bacon. Sprinkle with cheese and pecans.

4. Bake at 475° for 15 minutes or until edges are browned.

5. Combine cranberry sauce and next 3 ingredients in a small saucepan. Cook, stirring constantly, over medium heat 2 minutes or until thoroughly heated. Drizzle sauce over pizza.

CANDY CANE LANE SNACK MIX

MAKES 3 LB. HANDS-ON 15 MIN. TOTAL 35 MIN.

Package this treat in red-and-white striped containers lined with clear cellophane for a fun presentation.

Vegetable cooking spray
7 cups unsalted popped popcorn
3 cups mini-pretzel twists
2 cups shelled salted pistachios
Parchment paper
1¼ lb. vanilla candy coating, coarsely chopped
½ cup finely crushed red peppermint candy canes
1 cup white chocolate-peppermint baking chips
1 (5.8-oz.) container candy cane sprinkles

1. Coat a large bowl with cooking spray. Remove unpopped kernels from popcorn. Combine popcorn, pretzel twists, and pistachios in a large bowl. Line 2 jelly-roll pans with parchment paper.

2. Place candy coating in a medium saucepan. Cook over low heat 3 to 5 minutes or until coating melts, stirring occasionally. Stir in crushed peppermint candy. Pour melted candy mixture over popcorn mixture; toss to coat using 2 spatulas coated with cooking spray. Divide mixture between prepared jelly-roll pans. Sprinkle with white chocolate-peppermint baking chips, pressing gently to adhere. Top with candy cane sprinkles. Let stand 20 minutes or until firm. Break into pieces. Store in an airtight container in a cool place.

NOTE: We used Andes Peppermint Crunch Baking Chips.

ALMOND-COCONUT SWIRL CHOCOLATE BARK

MAKES 1¾ LB.   HANDS-ON 9 MIN.   TOTAL 39 MIN.

Parchment paper
3   cups bittersweet chocolate morsels
8   oz. white chocolate, chopped
⅓   cup sweetened flaked coconut, toasted
⅓   cup chopped natural almonds, toasted
⅓   cup chopped dried cherries

1. Line a baking sheet with parchment paper. Place bittersweet chocolate morsels in a microwave-safe bowl. Microwave at HIGH 1½ minutes or until melted, stirring at 30-second intervals until smooth. Using an offset spatula, spread melted chocolate into a 12- x 11-inch rectangle, about ¼ inch thick, on prepared baking sheet.
2. Place white chocolate in a microwave-safe bowl. Microwave at HIGH 1 minute or until melted, stirring at 15-second intervals until smooth. Spread white chocolate over bittersweet chocolate. Gently swirl chocolates using a skewer or the tip of a sharp knife.
3. Sprinkle coconut, almonds, and dried cherries over chocolate. Chill 30 minutes or until firm. Break into large chunks. Store in an airtight container.

holiday hints

CHILL OUT!

Our Almond-Coconut Swirl Chocolate Bark will be plenty firm after 30 minutes of chill time. However, if you're shipping the bark as a gift and want to ensure the chocolate won't melt (even slightly), let it set up in the freezer at least 2 to 3 hours before you break it into large chunks.

Crispy Espresso
Brownie Delights

Chocolate-Almond-
Coconut Bites

CRISPY ESPRESSO BROWNIE DELIGHTS

MAKES 30 SERVINGS
HANDS-ON 22 MIN.   TOTAL 3 HR., 2 MIN.

These two-layer brownie treats are chewy and crispy. Be sure to sprinkle the espresso beans quickly over the melted chocolate before it has a chance to harden.

Vegetable cooking spray
1   (18.75-oz.) package chocolate supreme brownie mix with chocolate syrup
⅓   cup vegetable oil
2   tsp. instant espresso
1   large egg
3   Tbsp. butter
1   (10-oz.) package miniature marshmallows
1   (7-oz.) jar marshmallow creme
6   cups chocolate-flavored crisp rice cereal
3   oz. bittersweet chocolate, chopped
3   oz. white chocolate, chopped
½   cup coarsely crushed chocolate-covered espresso beans

1. Preheat oven to 325°. Line 2 (9-inch) square pans with aluminum foil, allowing 2 to 3 inches to extend over sides. Lightly grease foil with cooking spray.

2. Prepare brownie mix, next 3 ingredients, and ¼ cup water according to package directions. Pour batter into 1 prepared pan. Bake at 325° for 30 minutes or until a wooden pick inserted in center comes out clean.

3. Meanwhile, place butter in a large microwave-safe bowl. Cover and microwave at HIGH 30 seconds or until melted. Stir in marshmallows and marshmallow creme. Microwave 1 to 2 more minutes or until melted and smooth, stirring at 30-second intervals. Add rice cereal, and quickly stir with a rubber spatula coated with cooking spray until cereal is coated.

4. Spoon cereal mixture into remaining prepared pan; press firmly into pan with fingers coated with cooking spray. Cool until brownies are done.

5. Remove cereal mixture from pan, retaining foil. Invert cereal mixture and foil onto hot brownies in pan. Firmly press bottom of 1 (9-inch) square pan on top of foil to adhere cereal layer to brownie layer. Cool completely (about 2 hours). Remove brownies from pan; discard foil. Cut into 30 small rectangles.

6. Place bittersweet chocolate and white chocolate in 2 separate microwave-safe bowls. Microwave each at HIGH 45 seconds or until melted and smooth, stirring at 15-second intervals. Drizzle desired amounts of melted chocolates over each rectangle; immediately sprinkle with crushed espresso beans. Chill 10 minutes or until chocolate is set.

NOTE: We tested with Ghirardelli Chocolate Supreme Brownie Mix and Cocoa Krispies.

CHOCOLATE-ALMOND-COCONUT BITES

MAKES 4 DOZEN   HANDS-ON 25 MIN.   TOTAL 1 HR., 53 MIN.

This is a very decadent take on mini chess pie bites. Adding the tropical flavors of coconut and almond to the mix makes them extra special.

½   cup sweetened flaked coconut
1   cup unsalted butter, softened
1   (8-oz.) package cream cheese, softened
2   cups all-purpose flour
½   cup almond meal
Vegetable cooking spray
2   large eggs, lightly beaten
1½   cups firmly packed brown sugar
2   Tbsp. butter, melted
2   tsp. vanilla extract
⅛   tsp. table salt
½   cup chopped almonds, toasted
½   cup semisweet mini-morsels
Maldon sea salt (optional)

1. Preheat oven to 350°. Place coconut in a single layer in a shallow pan.

2. Bake at 350° for 5 to 6 minutes or until toasted, stirring occasionally. Cool completely.

3. Place butter and cream cheese in a bowl. Beat at medium speed with an electric mixer until creamy. Reduce speed to low; gradually add flour and almond meal. Beat just until blended.

4. Shape dough by tablespoonfuls into 48 balls. Place balls on a baking sheet; cover and chill 30 minutes.

5. Preheat oven to 350°. Lightly grease 48 nonstick miniature muffin cups with cooking spray. Place 1 dough ball in each cup; press dough into bottom and up sides of cups, shaping each into a shell.

6. Whisk together eggs and next 4 ingredients in a medium bowl. Stir in almonds, mini-morsels, and coconut. Spoon filling evenly into pastry shells.

7. Bake at 350° for 18 to 20 minutes or until filling is set. Lightly sprinkle tops of tarts with sea salt while still hot, if desired. Cool in pans on wire racks 10 minutes. Carefully transfer tarts from muffin cups to wire racks. Cool completely (about 20 minutes). Store in an airtight container at room temperature up to 1 week.

CHOCOLATE-DIPPED GRAHAM CRACKERS

MAKES 6 DOZEN   HANDS-ON 33 MIN.   TOTAL 3 HR., 27 MIN.

For an extra-special touch to your gift, sprinkle graham crackers with the recipient's favorite chopped nuts or candies immediately after dipping the crackers in chocolate.

- 1½   cups all-purpose flour
- 1¼   cups whole wheat flour
- ⅔   cup firmly packed dark brown sugar
- 1   tsp. baking soda
- ½   tsp. table salt
- ¾   cup cold butter, cut up
- 3   Tbsp. honey
- 3   Tbsp. milk
- ½   tsp. vanilla extract
- Parchment paper
- 4   (4-oz.) semisweet chocolate baking bars, chopped
- Wax paper

1. Process first 5 ingredients in a food processor until blended. Add butter; pulse 10 times or until mixture resembles coarse meal. Add honey, milk, and vanilla; process 30 seconds or until dough forms a ball. Divide dough in half; shape each half into a 4-inch square, and wrap in plastic wrap. Chill 1 hour.

2. Preheat oven to 350°. Roll 1 portion of dough into a 12-inch square; cut into 36 (2-inch) squares. Place squares on a large baking sheet lined with parchment paper. Score each square crosswise down center; prick squares several times with a fork.

3. Bake at 350° for 14 minutes or until bottoms and edges are golden brown and crackers are set. Cool on pan 5 minutes. Transfer crackers to a wire rack. Cool completely (about 15 minutes). Meanwhile, repeat procedure with remaining portion of dough.

4. Place chopped chocolate in a microwave-safe bowl. Microwave at HIGH 1 minute or until chocolate melts, stirring every 15 seconds.

5. Dip half of each cracker in melted chocolate. Place dipped crackers on a work surface lined with wax paper. Let stand 1 hour or until chocolate is set.

SALTED BUTTERSCOTCH CARAMELS

MAKES 3 DOZEN   HANDS-ON 34 MIN.   TOTAL 2 HR., 34 MIN.

Wrap these decadently sweet bites in wax paper squares to give as gifts.

Vegetable cooking spray
1   cup whipping cream
1   tsp. white vinegar
¾   tsp. fine sea salt, divided
1   Tbsp. vanilla extract
¾   cup butter
1   cup granulated sugar
¾   cup firmly packed brown sugar
Wax paper

1. Line an 8-inch square pan with aluminum foil, allowing 2 to 3 inches to extend over sides. Lightly grease foil with cooking spray.

2. Bring whipping cream, vinegar, and ½ tsp. salt to a simmer in a medium saucepan over low heat. Remove from heat, and stir in vanilla.

3. Combine butter and next 2 ingredients in a 3-qt. heavy saucepan. Cook over medium heat 10 minutes or until sugar caramelizes and a candy thermometer registers 246° (firm ball stage), whisking just until sugars dissolve.

4. Remove pan from heat. Whisk in cream mixture until smooth. Return pan to heat, and cook, without stirring, until thermometer registers 246° (firm ball stage). Pour caramel into prepared pan. Sprinkle with remaining ¼ tsp. salt. Cool completely in pan on a wire rack (about 2 hours).

5. Remove caramel from pan; discard foil. Cut caramel into 1-inch squares. Wrap each square in wax paper, and store at room temperature.

CHEWY DARK CHOCOLATE–WALNUT COOKIES

MAKES ABOUT 8 DOZEN
HANDS-ON 40 MIN.   TOTAL 1 HR., 33 MIN.

These cookies will be lovely gifts for the holidays. Be sure to include the recipe, because your friends will want to make them, too.

2	cups granulated sugar
½	cup butter, softened
¼	cup shortening
2	large eggs
2	tsp. vanilla extract
2	cups all-purpose flour
¾	cup unsweetened cocoa
1	tsp. baking soda
½	tsp. table salt
1	(10-oz.) package dark chocolate morsels
1½	cups chopped walnut pieces
	Parchment paper
2	cups vanilla candy coating
½	cup sparkling sugar

1. Preheat oven to 350°. Combine first 3 ingredients in a bowl; beat at medium speed with an electric mixer until fluffy. Add eggs and vanilla, beating until blended.
2. Whisk together flour and next 3 ingredients. Gradually add flour mixture to butter mixture, beating at low speed until blended. Stir in chocolate morsels and walnuts.
3. Drop dough by 1½ teaspoonfuls onto parchment-paper lined baking sheets. Bake at 350° for 10 to 12 minutes. Transfer cookies to wire racks; cool completely (20 minutes).
4. Place candy coating in a microwave-safe bowl. Microwave at HIGH 1 minute, stirring at 15-second intervals until smooth. Cool melted candy slightly; spoon candy into a zip-top plastic freezer bag (do not seal). Snip 1 corner of bag to make a small hole. Drizzle melted candy over cooled cookies, and immediately sprinkle with sparkling sugar.

PRALINE PECAN GRANOLA WITH APPLES

MAKES 6½ CUPS
HANDS-ON 38 MIN.   TOTAL 1 HR., 8 MIN.

Granola is easy to prepare and usually yields a large amount, which makes it perfect for gift giving!

	Vegetable cooking spray
½	cup butter, melted
⅓	cup honey
3	Tbsp. brown sugar
1	tsp. vanilla extract
½	tsp. table salt
3	cups uncooked regular oats
2	cups coarsely chopped commercial praline pecans
¼	cup raw wheat germ
¼	cup roasted, salted, and shelled pepitas (pumpkin seeds)
1½	cups chopped dried apples

1. Preheat oven to 325°. Lightly grease a 15- x 10-inch jelly-roll pan with cooking spray. Stir together melted butter and next 4 ingredients in a large bowl. Add oats and next 3 ingredients, stirring until mixture is coated. Spread oat mixture on prepared pan.
2. Bake at 325° for 30 to 35 minutes or until golden brown, stirring every 10 minutes. Stir in apples. Cool completely in pan on a wire rack (about 30 minutes). Transfer to an airtight container and store at room temperature.

NOTE: We tested with Hoody's Deep South Praline Pecans.

holiday hints

QUICK COOKIE TREATS

We always like to have a stash of cookies we can bake in a flash for unexpected holiday guests or prepare as quick and easy gifts. Chewy Dark-Chocolate Walnut Cookies are just perfect. For each cookie, simply roll 1½ tsp. dough into a ball, place balls on a baking sheet, and freeze. Once they're frozen, transfer the dough balls to a zip-top plastic freezer bag. When the occasion calls for quick cookies, pull out your frozen stockpile, let it thaw at room temperature, and bake as directed.

BUTTERSCOTCH-PECAN PRETZEL BRITTLE

MAKES ABOUT 1 LB.   HANDS-ON 8 MIN.   TOTAL 50 MIN.

This crispy, salty, sweet snack is sure to become a family holiday favorite.

Parchment paper
5   cups mini-pretzel twists
⅔   cup butterscotch morsels
1   cup chopped pecans, divided
¼   cup unsalted butter
¼   cup maple syrup
¼   cup sugar

1. Preheat oven to 350°. Line an 18- x 13-inch rimmed baking sheet with parchment paper. Place pretzel twists, butterscotch morsels, and ⅔ cup pecans in a medium bowl.
2. Combine butter, syrup, and sugar in a small saucepan. Cook, stirring constantly, over medium heat 3 to 4 minutes or until butter melts and sugar dissolves. Pour over pretzel mixture, tossing to coat. Spread coated pretzel mixture in an even layer on prepared pan (pretzels will overlap). Sprinkle with remaining ⅓ cup pecans.
3. Bake at 350° for 12 minutes or until lightly browned. Cool completely (about 30 minutes). Break into pieces.

HAZELNUT BRITTLE

MAKES ABOUT 1¼ LB.   HANDS-ON 23 MIN.   TOTAL 38 MIN.

Old-fashioned peanut brittle is updated and modernized in this recipe with hazelnuts and sea salt. Drizzle with dark or milk chocolate for an especially rich treat.

Shortening
1   cup sugar
⅓   cup light corn syrup
1½   cups roasted skinned hazelnuts, coarsely chopped
2   Tbsp. butter
1   tsp. vanilla extract
½   tsp. baking soda
½   tsp. coarse sea salt, divided

1. Grease (with shortening) a 15- x 10-inch jelly-roll pan. Bring sugar, corn syrup, and ¼ cup water to a boil over medium heat in a large, heavy saucepan, stirring just until sugar dissolves. Boil, without stirring, 6 minutes or until a candy thermometer registers 270°. Stir in hazelnuts and cook 3 minutes or until thermometer registers 300°. Remove from heat and stir in butter, next 2 ingredients, and ¼ tsp. sea salt.
2. Working quickly, spread mixture in a thin layer in prepared pan. Sprinkle with remaining ¼ tsp. sea salt. Let stand 15 minutes or until hardened. Break into pieces.

PEPPER-ONION RELISH

MAKES 8 (½-PT.) JARS
HANDS-ON 27 MIN.   TOTAL 1 HR., 37 MIN.

This sweet and savory relish will be everyone's favorite gift. Give it in a basket with artisan crackers and cream cheese for an instant appetizer.

5½   cups chopped red bell pepper
3   cups chopped sweet onion
2   cups sugar
1½   cups white vinegar
½   cup seeded and chopped jalapeño pepper
1   tsp. table salt
½   tsp. ground red pepper
4   garlic cloves, minced
3   (14½-oz.) cans diced tomatoes, drained

Bring all ingredients to a boil in a Dutch oven; reduce heat, and simmer, uncovered, 45 minutes or until the consistency of chunky tomato sauce, stirring often. Remove from heat and cool 30 minutes. Divide relish among 8 (½-pt.) sterilized canning jars. Cover and refrigerate up to 1 week.

PEAR-APPLE CHUTNEY

MAKES 9 (½-PT.) JARS
HANDS-ON 20 MIN.   TOTAL 2 HR., 10 MIN.

Friends and family will thoroughly enjoy this versatile chutney. Pair with cream cheese and crackers for a sweet appetizer, spoon over grilled pork, or use as a spread on a grilled cheese for a savory sandwich.

2   cups granulated sugar
1   cup firmly packed light brown sugar
1   cup chopped onion
1   cup sweetened dried cranberries
¾   cup apple cider
¾   cup apple cider vinegar
¼   cup fresh orange juice (1 large orange)
2   Tbsp. grated fresh ginger
½   tsp. table salt
¼   tsp. ground cinnamon
6   Bartlett pears (3 lb.), peeled and chopped
5   Fuji apples (3 lb.), peeled and chopped

1. Bring all ingredients to a boil in a large Dutch oven; reduce heat, and simmer, uncovered, 1½ hours or until thickened and glossy, stirring occasionally. Remove from heat; cool slightly.
2. Pour hot chutney into 9 (½-pt.) sterilized canning jars. Cover and refrigerate up to 2 weeks.

FESTIVE POMEGRANATE-CRANBERRY SYRUP

MAKES 3¼ CUPS
HANDS-ON 16 MIN.   TOTAL 2 HR., 56 MIN.

This versatile syrup is great on pancakes and waffles, but also does double duty to sweeten holiday libations.

3   cups cranberry juice cocktail
2   cups unsweetened pomegranate juice
2   cups fresh cranberries
1½ cups light corn syrup
1   cup sugar
4   star anise
2   (3-inch) cinnamon sticks

1. Bring all ingredients to a boil in a medium saucepan over medium-high heat, stirring until sugar dissolves. Reduce heat, and simmer, uncovered, 40 minutes or until reduced to 4 cups.
2. Pour mixture through a fine wire-mesh strainer into a bowl. Discard solids. Divide mixture among 4 decorative bottles. Cover and chill 2 hours or until cold. Refrigerate in airtight containers for up to 2 weeks.

LEMON-GINGER-BASIL SYRUP

MAKES 6 (½-PT.) JARS
HANDS-ON 5 MIN.   TOTAL 1 HR., 20 MIN.

Stir this sweet, tangy syrup into homemade seltzer, or mix into vodka or gin for a refreshing cocktail. It can also be brushed over pound cake or angel food cake to sweeten up your favorite dessert.

3½ cups lemon slices (4 lemons)
3   cups sugar
1   (3-inch) piece fresh ginger, peeled and sliced
10 basil leaves

1. Bring first 3 ingredients and 4 cups water to a boil in a medium saucepan; reduce heat, and simmer, uncovered, 5 minutes, stirring occasionally. Remove from heat; stir in basil. Let stand, uncovered, 20 minutes. Pour syrup through a fine wire-mesh strainer into a bowl; discard solids. Cool completely (about 45 minutes).
2. Pour mixture into 6 (½-pt.) sterilized canning jars. Cover and refrigerate up to 3 weeks.

LEMON-GINGER-BASIL SPARKLING WATER: For each serving, gently stir ¼ cup syrup into 1 cup sparkling water. Serve over ice.

MEXICAN HOT COCOA MIX

MAKES 28 SERVINGS   HANDS-ON 8 MIN.   TOTAL 8 MIN.

Mexican hot chocolate gets a hint of heat from ground red pepper and a little spiciness from cinnamon. For an even more authentic flavor, look for Mexican brands of chocolate found at specialty markets or in the ethnic food aisle at the supermarket.

2   cups instant nonfat dry milk
1¾ cups granulated sugar
1⅓ cups Dutch process cocoa
¾   cup powdered sugar
½   tsp. ground cinnamon
¼   tsp. ground red pepper
Pinch of kosher salt
3   cups dark chocolate morsels

Stir together first 7 ingredients in a large bowl until blended. Stir in chocolate morsels. Spoon mixture into an airtight container. Store at room temperature.

FOR EACH SERVING: Combine 1 cup hot milk and ¼ cup Mexican Hot Cocoa Mix, stirring until chocolate morsels melt. Top each serving with whipped cream and a cinnamon stick, if desired.

holiday hints
FIT TO BE TIED

You put a lot of love into the preparation of these gifts from your kitchen, and they should look as fabulous as they taste. Trim your treats with complementary culinary items or ingredients. For example, loop cinnamon sticks or star anise on pretty ribbons, or use twine to tie on tools like a vintage silver chutney spoon as part of the gift.

Love it? GET IT!

Many items pictured in the book are one-of-a-kind or no longer available—we've listed similar items when possible. Source information is current at the time of publication. If an item is not listed, its source is unknown.

Pages 10-27: Sweet Home Holiday

Greenery—tree, garland, and wreaths: Gardens of the Blue Ridge, www.gardensoftheblueridge.com; **wrapping paper:** Minted, www.minted.com; **alabaster tree ornaments, galvanized pedestals:** Roost, www.roostco.com; **handmade patchwork stockings and burlap bag ornaments:** Chelsea Antique Mall, www.chelseaantiquemallal.com; **galvanized wreath on wood:** Park Hill from Bromberg's, www.brombergs.com; **antique sled:** Europe to You, www.europe2you.com; **red and white dishes, dessert plates** "Sevilla" by Vista Alegre, www.vistaalegre.bridgecatalog.com; **tree skirt, red felt reindeer ornaments, stocking wall pocket:** D. Stevens LLC, www.dstevensllc.com; **wooly snowflakes in white:** Foreside Home & Garden, www.foresidehomeandgarden.com; **galvanized buckets with red scallop edge:** Sugarboo Designs, www.sugaboodesigns.com; **wooden tags:** HomArt, www.homart.com; **pewter serving pieces:** Match from Bromberg's, www.brombergs.com; **faux ribbon candy trees:** Hobby Lobby, www.hobbylobby.com; **red and cream throw:** Serena & Lily, www.serenaandlily.com; **wooden pedestals:** Europe to You, www.europe2you.com; **red leather sleigh bells:** Christmas Tree Shops, www.christmastreeshops.com; **natural linen napkins:** Libeco, www.libeco.com; **star plates, pie plate:** Eigen Arts, www.eigenarts.com; **jolly letters:** Design Legacy, www.design-legacy.com; **trees pillow:** Greystone Antiques, www.facebook.com/greystone.antiques; **lanterns, fireplace screen:** At Home, www.athome.com

Pages 30-45: Merry and Mod

Flocked tree: Beavers Christmas Tree Farm, www.beaverschristmastreefarm.com; **square wreaths:** Gardens of the Blue Ridge, www.gardensoftheblueridge.com; **wrapping paper:** Minted, www.minted.com; One Kings Lane, www.onekingslane.com; Paper Source, www.papersource.com; **flowers—dusty miller, brunia, snow on the mountain, white tulips, white ranunculus, and white hydrangea:** Davis Wholesale Florist, Inc., www.daviswholesaleflorist.com; **tree topper:** Leaf & Petal, www.leafnpetal.com; **ornaments:** Roost, www.roostco.com; Sullivans, www.sullivangift.com; Davis Wholesale Florist, Inc., www.daviswholesaleflorist.com; **ribbons:** Midori, www.midoriribbon.com; Hobby Lobby, www.hobbylobby.com; Michaels, www.michaels.com;

Smith's Variety; **throws and pillows, gold stripe, dot cocktail glasses, metallic vases:** West Elm, www.westelm.com; **tall turquoise vase:** Tuesday Morning, www.tuesdaymorning.com; **nailhead side chairs, smoky martini glasses:** HomeGoods, www.homegoods.com; **marble circles on stands:** Gold Leaf Design Group, www.goldleafdesigngroup.com; **tabletop brass accent "Scoppio Sphere":** Z Gallerie, www.zgallerie.com; **tall green wine glasses:** vintage from Tricia's Treasures, www.triciastreasures.us; **bar cart:** vintage from King's House Antiques, www.kingshouseantiques.com; **striped shaker and decanter:** vintage from Soho Retro, www.shophomewood.com; **dishes:** Fortunata, www.fortunatainc.com; Gleena, www.gleena.com; Kate Spade, www.katespade.com; Roost, www.roostco.com; **kidney-shaped nesting tables, coffee table:** Blue Ocean Traders, www.blueoceantraders.com; **starburst medallion:** Village Firefly, www.thevillagefirefly.com; **geometric shapes plates:** Fortunata, www.fortunatainc.com; **striped cheese platter:** Eigen Arts, www.eigenarts.com

Pages 46-61: A Christmas Story

Greenery—tree, garland, and wreaths: Gardens of the Blue Ridge, www.gardensoftheblueridge.com; **wrapping paper:** Paper Source, www.papersource.com; Smith's Variety; **ornaments and tree garlands:** Midwest-CBK, www.mwcbk.com; Kurt S. Adler, www.kurtadler.com; Sullivans, www.sullivangift.com; Hobby Lobby, www.hobbylobby.com; World Market, www.worldmarket.com; Lancaster Home & Holiday, www.lancasterhomeandholiday.com; Roost, roostco.com; **snowballs:** Shea's Wildflower Company, www.sheaswildflowers.com; **multi-colored fringe tree skirt and stockings:** Arcadia Home, www.arcadiahomeinc.com; **ribbons, tree stand with paper cones:** Wisteria, www.wisteria.com; **pillows:** Pottery Barn, www.potterybarn.com; **candles:** Christmas Tree Shops, www.christmastreeshops.com; **white mini trees and wreaths:** Lancaster Home & Holiday, www.lancasterhomeandholiday.com; **antique bowling pins, red metal firewood bin:** vintage from Chelsea Antique Mall, www.chelseaantiquemallal.com; **red metal truck:** Park Hill Collection, www.parkhillcollection.com; **dishes:** Azulina Ceramics, www.azulina.com; **turquoise rolling tiered stand:** Foreside Home & Garden, www.foresidehomeandgarden.com; **ribbon candy:** Hammond's Candies, www.hammondscandies.com; **fireplace screen:** At Home, www.athome.com; **curtain fabric:** Ex Voto Vintage, www.exvotovintage.com

www.exvotovintage.com; **stockings and pillows:** Paige Albright Orientals, www.paigealbrightorientals.com; **fireplace screen:** At Home, www.athome.com; **crown ornament:** Aux Belles Choses, www.abcneworleans.com

Pages 62-77: High Tea and Tinsel

Greenery—tree, garland, and wreaths: Gardens of the Blue Ridge, www.gardensoftheblueridge.com; **crystals, antique silver, crown topper:** Tricia's Treasures, www.triciastreasures.us; **large gold sphere ornaments:** Christmas Tree Shops, www.christmastreeshops.com; **linens:** Chelsea Antique Mall, www.chelseaantiquemallal.com; **tartan napkins, red cocktail napkins:** Table Matters, www.table-matters.com; **tiered crystal and silver server:** Baccarat, us.baccarat.com; **gold Champagne flutes:** Anthropologie, www.anthropologie.com; **crown votives:** Wisteria, www.wisteria.com; **gold bowl with pears:** Montes Doggett, www.montesdoggett.com; **ribbon:** Martha Stewart Everyday, shop.marthastewart.com; Michaels, www.michaels.com; **wrapping paper:** Smith's Variety; **teacups:** antique and Bromberg's, www.brombergs.com; **locket:** Ex Voto Vintage,

Pages 78-85: Hollywood Glam New Year's Eve

Greenery—tree: Gardens of the Blue Ridge, www.gardensoftheblueridge.com; **bar cart, ice bucket, large silver leaf tray, star garland:** West Elm, www.westelm.com; **glass serving platter:** Annieglass at Bromberg's, www.brombergs.com; **silver metallic napkin, gold flatware:** Table Matters, www.table-matters.com; **stemless Champagne flute:** Roost: www.roostco.com; **rug:** Paige Albright Orientals, www.paigealbrightorientals.com; **fireplace screen:** At Home, www.athome.com; **rock candy trees:** Sugar, www.shopmountainbrook.com/sugar; **mirror:** Tricia's Treasures, www.triciastreasures.us; **ornaments:** Jim Marvin Collections, www.jimmarvin.net; Abbott Collection, www.abbottcollection.com; **dessert plates:** Canvas Home, www.canvashomestore.com

Thanks
TO THESE CONTRIBUTORS

Thanks to the following businesses

Anthropologie	Ex Voto Vintage	Lamb's Ears, Ltd.	Sur La Table
At Home	Flowerbuds	Michaels	Table Matters
Attic Antiques	Greystone Antiques and Marketplace	Oak Street Garden Shop	Tricia's Treasures
Bromberg's		Paige Albright Orientals	West Elm
Chelsea Antique Mall	Hall's Birmingham Wholesale Florist	Paper Source	Williams-Sonoma
Collier's Nursery	Hanna Antiques Mall	Pottery Barn	World Market
Crate & Barrel	Henhouse Antiques	Smith's Variety	
Davis Wholesale Florist	Hobby Lobby	Sugar	

Thanks to the following homeowners

The Adams Family
The Ricketts Family
The Starling Family

The Statham Family
The Taylor Family

General Index

Metric Equivalent

The recipes that appear in this cookbook use the standard United States method for measuring liquid and dry or solid ingredients (teaspoons, tablespoons, and cups). The information in the following charts is provided to help cooks outside the U.S. successfully use these recipes. All equivalents are approximate.

Metric Equivalents for Different Types of Ingredients

A standard cup measure of a dry or solid ingredient will vary in weight depending on the type of ingredient. A standard cup of liquid is the same volume for any type of liquid. Use the following chart when converting standard cup measures to grams (weight) or milliliters (volume).

Standard Cup	Fine Powder (ex. flour)	Grain (ex. rice)	Granular (ex. sugar)	Liquid Solids (ex. butter)	Liquid (ex. milk)
1	140 g	150 g	190 g	200 g	240 ml
¾	105 g	113 g	143 g	150 g	180 ml
⅔	93 g	100 g	125 g	133 g	160 ml
½	70 g	75 g	95 g	100 g	120 ml
⅓	47 g	50 g	63 g	67 g	80 ml
¼	35 g	38 g	48 g	50 g	60 ml
⅛	18 g	19 g	24 g	25 g	30 ml

Useful Equivalents for Dry Ingredients by Weight

(To convert ounces to grams, multiply the number of ounces by 30.)

1 oz	=	1/16 lb	=	30 g
4 oz	=	¼ lb	=	120 g
8 oz	=	½ lb	=	240 g
12 oz	=	¾ lb	=	360 g
16 oz	=	1 lb	=	480 g

Useful Equivalents for Length

(To convert inches to centimeters, multiply the number of inches by 2.5.)

1 in				=	2.5 cm		
6 in	=	½ ft		=	15 cm		
12 in	=	1 ft		=	30 cm		
36 in	=	3 ft	=	1 yd	=	90 cm	
40 in				=	100 cm	=	1 m

Useful Equivalents for Liquid Ingredients by Volume

¼ tsp					=	1 ml	
½ tsp					=	2 ml	
1 tsp					=	5 ml	
3 tsp	=	1 Tbsp		=	½ fl oz	=	15 ml
		2 Tbsp	=	⅛ cup	=	1 fl oz	=	30 ml
		4 Tbsp	=	¼ cup	=	2 fl oz	=	60 ml
		5⅓ Tbsp	=	⅓ cup	=	3 fl oz	=	80 ml
		8 Tbsp	=	½ cup	=	4 fl oz	=	120 ml
		10⅔ Tbsp	=	⅔ cup	=	5 fl oz	=	160 ml
		12 Tbsp	=	¾ cup	=	6 fl oz	=	180 ml
		16 Tbsp	=	1 cup	=	8 fl oz	=	240 ml
		1 pt	=	2 cups	=	16 fl oz	=	480 ml
		1 qt	=	4 cups	=	32 fl oz	=	960 ml
					33 fl oz	=	1000 ml	= 1 l

Useful Equivalents for Cooking/Oven Temperatures

	Fahrenheit	Celsius	Gas Mark
Freeze water	32° F	0° C	
Room temperature	68° F	20° C	
Boil water	212° F	100° C	
Bake	325° F	160° C	3
	350° F	180° C	4
	375° F	190° C	5
	400° F	200° C	6
	425° F	220° C	7
	450° F	230° C	8
Broil			Grill

Recipe Index

©2015 Time Inc. Books
1271 Avenue of the Americas, New York, NY 10020

Southern Living® is a registered trademark of Time Inc. Lifestyle Group. All rights reserved. No part of this book may be reproduced in any form or by any means without the prior written permission of the publisher, excepting brief quotations in connection with reviews written specifically for inclusion in magazines or newpapers, or limited excerpts strictly for personal use.

ISBN-13: 978-0-8487-4467-0
ISBN-10: 0-8487-4467-5
ISSN: 0747-7791

Printed in the United States of America
First Printing 2015

Oxmoor House
Editorial Director: Anja Schmidt
Creative Director: Felicity Keane
Art Director: Christopher Rhoads
Executive Photography Director: Iain Bagwell
Executive Food Director: Grace Parisi
Photo Editor: Kellie Lindsey
Managing Editor: Elizabeth Tyler Austin
Assistant Managing Editor: Jeanne de Lathouder

Christmas with Southern Living 2015
Editor: Sarah A. Gleim
Assistant Project Editor: Lacie Pinyan
Senior Designer: Melissa Clark
Assistant Designer: Allison Sperando Potter
Assistant Test Kitchen Manager: Alyson Moreland Haynes
Recipe Developers and Testers: Julia Levy, Stefanie Maloney, Callie Nash, Karen Rankin
Food Stylists: Nathan Carrabba, Victoria E. Cox, Margaret Monroe Dickey, Catherine Crowell Steele
Senior Photographer: Hélène Dujardin
Senior Photo Stylists: Kay E. Clarke, Mindi Shapiro Levine
Senior Production Manager: Greg A. Amason
Assistant Production Director: Sue Chodakiewicz

Contributors
Executive Editor: Katherine Cobbs
Junior Designer: AnnaMaria Jacob
Recipe Editor: Julie Christopher
Recipe Developers and Testers: Tamara Goldis, R.D.; Leah Van Deren
Copy Editor: Jasmine Hodges
Proofreaders: Rebecca Brennan, Rebecca Henderson
Indexer: Mary Ann Laurens
Fellows: Laura Arnold, Kylie Dazzo, Nicole Fisher, Loren Lorenzo, Anna Ramia, Caroline Smith, Amanda Widis
Food Stylist Assistant: Angela Schmidt
Photographers: Stephen Devries, Becky Luigart-Stayner
Photo Stylists: Mary Clayton Carl, Missie Neville Crawford, Lydia DeGaris Pursell
Assistant Photo Stylist: Allison Belcher

Time Inc. Books
Publisher: Margot Schupf
Vice President, Finance: Vandana Patel
Executive Director, Marketing Services: Carol Pittard
Executive Director, Business Development: Suzanne Albert
Executive Director, Marketing: Susan Hettleman
Assistant General Counsel: Simone Procas
Assistant Project Manager: Allyson Angle

Cover: Chocolate Peppermint Layer Cake, page 148

Back Cover (clockwise from top left): Short Rib Pot Pies, page 121; Coconut-Citrus Pavlova, page 142; Stockings, page 10; Pink Bunny Cupcakes and Peppermint Swirl Hot Chocolate, page 51; Presents, page 59

Holiday
PLANNER

This handy planner will help you stay on track
all season long. From decorating and table-setting tips
to gift and card lists, everything you need to plan
the perfect holiday is at your fingertips.

November 2015

Sunday	Monday	Tuesday	Wednesday
1	2	3	4
8	9	10	11
15	16	17	18
22	23	24	25
29	30		

Thursday	Friday	Saturday
5	6	7
12	13	14
19	20	21
Thanksgiving 26	27	28

ULTIMATE HOLIDAY CHECKLIST

If you're like many Southerners, you probably started your Christmas shopping months ago. But now it's time to really start planning, so make this your best holiday ever with our go-to checklist!

Early to mid-November

○ Make a master gift list, and start shopping. Don't forget to note homemade food gifts you're planning for neighbors and teachers, as well as gratuities or gift cards you plan to give to service-related people, such as the babysitter, hairdresser, mailman, garbage collectors, etc.

○ Stock up on stamps, wrapping supplies, and cooking/baking staples.

○ Order holiday cards.

Late November (after Thanksgiving)

○ Plan to shop any Black Friday sales for big-ticket items with big discounts.

○ Start addressing holiday cards.

○ Take decorations out of storage.

Early December

○ Plan holiday meals and menus, and place orders at any local shops or bakeries.

○ Start decorating! Trim the tree, and put up the wreaths, garlands, and any other holiday decor.

○ Finish your holiday shopping, wrapping gifts as you buy them.

○ Mail holiday cards.

Mid-December

○ Mail gifts for out-of-town family and friends.

○ Get your house ready for guests by tidying up any guest rooms and bathrooms.

○ Hit the grocery store for all nonperishable foods.

○ Start cooking! Prepare any make-ahead dishes, and freeze them.

The Week Before Christmas

○ Set the table, putting out all serving dishes and utensils you plan to use.

○ Go to the grocery store for all fresh or perishable items.

○ Finish any cooking that can be done in advance.

○ Relax and enjoy your holiday!

December 2015

Sunday	Monday	Tuesday	Wednesday
		1	2
6	7	8	9
13	14	15	16
20	21	22	23
27	28	29	30

Thursday	Friday	Saturday
3	4	5
10	11	12
17	18	19
Christmas Eve 24	Christmas 25	Boxing Day 26
New Year's Eve 31		

CHOOSING THE RIGHT CHRISTMAS TREE

There's no substitution for a real Christmas tree. Artificial trees may be convenient, but how many memories can you create around a plastic tree that you dragged out of the attic? Plus, part of the joy of Christmas is the smell of a fresh-cut tree. Follow these steps to finding your perfect match.

Know Your Maximum Size

○ To calculate your maximum tree size, measure the height of your ceiling and then subtract 1 foot. This will allow ample room for your topper. Keep girth in mind, too: The smaller the room, the skinnier the tree should be.

Check for Freshness on the Lot

○ Nothing kills that Christmas mood quite like a tree with no needles. Run your fingers down a branch before you buy. All needles should stay intact, and your hand should smell like your evergreen of choice. Gentle shaking should also result in very little needle drop. If not, keep looking.

Even with diligent care, cut trees only last about 10 days. Your best bet is to cut your own from a farm or to purchase one from a store or lot that offers trees harvested within days of delivery. High prices don't always guarantee freshness, and rock-bottom tags often yield bad results, too.

Recut the Trunk on an Angle

○ Once home, you're probably ready to decorate—but not before re-cutting the trunk about 1 inch above the butt end to aid in water absorption. If you don't have a saw, most tree lots will do this for you. Get your tree into a bucket of water within an hour of cutting, or the pores will seal and your effort will be in vain.

If the tree is fresh-cut from a farm, put it in the stand. Otherwise, soak it in a bucket of water outside overnight. You can also spray it down with a hose to remove debris and help hydrate the needles.

Decorating PLANNER

Here's a list of details and finishing touches you can use to
tailor a picture-perfect house this holiday season.

Decorative materials needed

from the yard ....

....

from around the house ....

....

from the store ....

....

other ....

Holiday decorations

for the table ....

....

for the door ....

....

for the mantel ....

....

for the staircase ....

....

other ....

RING IN THE SEASON

Nothing is more welcoming during the holidays than a striking door wreath. You'll love these
four versions, because each offers an elegant twist to the classic evergreen wreath.

FLOCKED

Long, slender pinecones, such as those of a white pine, work best for this new take on a Southern holiday
classic—the pinecone wreath.

Materials you'll need:

9   flat wooden paint stirrers

12-inch green wire wreath form

clippers

Gorilla Glue

long, thin pinecones

artificial snow spray

1. Make wreath base by weaving six wooden paint stirrers through
the edges of a wire wreath form (like the rays of a sunburst). Cut
remaining three stirrers in half. Place cut stirrers on top of already-
attached stirrers in the center of the wreath to form a hexagon.
Secure wooden stirrers with Gorilla Glue per label directions. Let dry.

2. Glue a pinecone to the top of each stirrer so the tip points out.
Glue pinecones to the wire frame between each stirrer.

3. Add pinecones at an angle to the sides of each stirrer. Cut more
pinecones into disks and use to fill in gaps, gluing into place.

4. Spray the wreath with several coats of artificial snow, letting it dry
between applications.

MOSS

Soothing hues and luscious textures set the tone for an elegant holiday. Scout out shady corners of your garden for lush mats of moss to create this easy wreath. Supplement with store-bought moss as needed.

Materials you'll need:

18-inch FloraCraft straw wreath

4   bags of sheet moss or moss from the garden

hot-melt glue gun

3   bags of variety-pack moss (such as mood, reindeer, or lichen) or mosses and lichens gathered from the yard

florist pins

1   yard of 3-inch-wide satin ribbon

1. Cover a straw wreath with sheets of moss, hot-gluing into place.

2. Strategically place large, thick pieces of moss (such as mood moss) next. Hot-glue in place, and secure with florist pins. Fill in with small patches of reindeer moss and lichen.

3. Loop satin ribbon over the bottom of the wreath, and tie it in a knot.

SUCCULENTS

A living succulent wreath can be displayed as a centerpiece, tied to the back of a chair, or hung on an interior wall. And with regular watering and bright light, it can live for years.

Materials you'll need:

1   (13-inch) Living Wreath Sphagnum Moss Form (amazon.com)

bucket of water large enough to soak wreath

awl or chopstick

40   (1½-inch-diameter) pots or cuttings of succulents

florist paddle wire

2   yards of 2½-inch-wide decorative satin ribbon

1. Soak wreath form in a bucket of water so sphagnum moss and inner soil are saturated. Lift from bucket, and let excess water drain.

2. Punch a hole in the wreath form with an awl or chopstick. Insert succulents. (If using potted plants rather than cuttings, make hole larger, remove excess soil from roots, and squeeze remaining soil to make insertion easier.) Once succulents are planted, water well by submerging in a bucket of water. Lift and drain.

3. Loop florist paddle wire over the wreath to support the weight when hung, and then cover with decorative satin ribbon, tying a bow at the top.

4. Water as needed, letting wreath get slightly dry between waterings.

TREE FORM

A tree-shaped wreath made of fresh greenery offers an alternative to the traditional round wreath without sacrificing the fragrance.

Materials you'll need:

bamboo stake, cut into 3 pieces: 2 (15-inch) lengths and 1 (12-inch) length

clippers

florist paddle wire

Gorilla Glue

mixed greenery and twigs

9   small pinecones

1   foot of 1-inch-wide satin ribbon

1. Form a triangle with bamboo stake pieces. Secure ends by wrapping with florist paddle wire. Add a drop of Gorilla Glue to wrapped ends to reinforce.

2. Create 5-inch-long bundles of mixed greenery, and secure to frame with florist paddle wire. For a full wreath, alternate bundles on the inside and outside of the frame while working in one direction. Foliage should point up. At the bottom of the wreath, work out from the center. Wrap wire around pinecones, and tie them to the wreath to embellish, if desired.

3. Fashion a trunk by wiring together twigs, and then wire the bundle onto the base of the wreath. Wrap the bundle with ribbon, and tie in a bow.

Party PLANNER

Stay on top of your party plans with our time-saving menu organizer.

GUESTS	WHAT THEY'RE BRINGING	SERVING PIECES NEEDED

.... ☐ appetizer ☐ beverage ☐ bread ☐ main dish ☐ side dish ☐ dessert ....

.... ☐ appetizer ☐ beverage ☐ bread ☐ main dish ☐ side dish ☐ dessert ....

.... ☐ appetizer ☐ beverage ☐ bread ☐ main dish ☐ side dish ☐ dessert ....

.... ☐ appetizer ☐ beverage ☐ bread ☐ main dish ☐ side dish ☐ dessert ....

.... ☐ appetizer ☐ beverage ☐ bread ☐ main dish ☐ side dish ☐ dessert ....

.... ☐ appetizer ☐ beverage ☐ bread ☐ main dish ☐ side dish ☐ dessert ....

.... ☐ appetizer ☐ beverage ☐ bread ☐ main dish ☐ side dish ☐ dessert ....

.... ☐ appetizer ☐ beverage ☐ bread ☐ main dish ☐ side dish ☐ dessert ....

.... ☐ appetizer ☐ beverage ☐ bread ☐ main dish ☐ side dish ☐ dessert ....

.... ☐ appetizer ☐ beverage ☐ bread ☐ main dish ☐ side dish ☐ dessert ....

.... ☐ appetizer ☐ beverage ☐ bread ☐ main dish ☐ side dish ☐ dessert ....

.... ☐ appetizer ☐ beverage ☐ bread ☐ main dish ☐ side dish ☐ dessert ....

.... ☐ appetizer ☐ beverage ☐ bread ☐ main dish ☐ side dish ☐ dessert ....

.... ☐ appetizer ☐ beverage ☐ bread ☐ main dish ☐ side dish ☐ dessert ....

.... ☐ appetizer ☐ beverage ☐ bread ☐ main dish ☐ side dish ☐ dessert ....

Party Guest List

Grocery List

Party To-Do List

CHRISTMAS *Dinner* PLANNER

Use this space to create a menu, to-do list, and guest list for your special holiday celebration.

Menu Ideas

....
....
....
....
....
....
....

Dinner To-Do List

....
....
....
....
....
....
....

Christmas Dinner Guest List

....
....
....
....
....
....
....
....
....

SET A STYLISH TABLE

Take inspiration from these festive table settings for every holiday meal,
from a casual family breakfast to a glamorous fireside dinner.

Formal Holiday Lunch

Give a midday gathering the Midas touch with a table laden with golden accents. This luxe look elevates lunch to a must-attend event. Utilize wooden trays as chargers beneath gold china and gold-edged glass dessert plates. Vintage fabric pouches can hold place cards and do double duty as party favors for your guests.

Enchanting Dinner Party

Create a cozy woodland setting with birch log candleholders embellished with moss, twigs, and berries. Add faux bois china and hints of gleaming gold to make the rustic tableau a little more refined, and scatter glass acorn ornaments across the table for added shine.

Christmas Eve Celebration

Add drama to a classic holiday china pattern with an amped-up tablescape of red accents. Create a stunning focal point with red ribbons radiating from a centerpiece of roses and wrapped peppermint candies. Red chargers, napkins, stemware, and even red rental chairs will add modern flair and pop against a bright white tablecloth. Tape mini candy canes together to form petite easels for place cards.

Festive Christmas Breakfast

For a laid-back family gathering, leave a pretty wooden table uncovered to keep the look unfussy. Use simple white china in interesting shapes, and rely on a mix of textures, like velvet, linen, and wood, for maximum impact. Make your own place cards with crafts store basics: Back a simple white name card with a second larger patterned card, thread a wide red velvet ribbon between the two on a plate, and your place settings will look like holiday gifts.

New Year's Eve Cocktail Supper

Layer gold-rimmed china with mint green and pink for an unexpected but fresh holiday palette. Add a scattering of metallic confetti atop each place setting for a festive touch. Cut a slit in the tops of Champagne corks to serve as fun place card holders. For a final flourish, have a calligrapher pen the names of dinner guests on place cards.

STOCK A SPIRITED BAR CART

The holidays are the time to ditch the late-night dives and hibernate
with family at home instead—and stocking the ultimate drink cart means
more than supplying it with libations.

Have Cheese Straws at the Ready

These savory snacks freeze and thaw with ease, making them ideal small bites to stockpile.

Include Fresh Flowers

Vibrant red amaryllis contrast well with glass and metal bar carts. Arrange flowers in shakers or ice buckets for a clever touch.

Leave Your Mark

Wooden monogram stir sticks add a functional focal point and deviate from the standard monogram napkins you expect to see.

Skip the Paper Napkins

Disposable napkins are cheaper up front, but you save in the long run with cotton. At Christmas, outfit your bar cart with tartan linens.

Opt for Vintage Wares

Handsome glasses instantly elevate a cart's look. Use mismatched finds for a more storied display than a straight-from-the-box set.

Serve Southern Staples

Stay true to your roots with Southern-made essentials such as Elmer T. Lee bourbon (Kentucky), Corsair gin (Tennessee), and Jack Rudy tonic (South Carolina).

Gifts & Greetings

Keep up with family and friends' sizes, jot down gift ideas, and record purchases in this convenient chart. Also, use it to keep track of addresses for your Christmas card list.

Gift List and Size Charts

NAME/SIZES	GIFT PURCHASED/MADE	SENT

name ....

jeans_____ shirt_____ sweater_____ jacket_____ shoes_____ belt__

blouse_____ skirt_____ slacks_____ dress_____ suit_____ coat_____

pajamas_____ robe_____ hat_____ gloves_____ ring_____

name ....

jeans_____ shirt_____ sweater_____ jacket_____ shoes_____ belt__

blouse_____ skirt_____ slacks_____ dress_____ suit_____ coat_____

pajamas_____ robe_____ hat_____ gloves_____ ring_____

name ....

jeans_____ shirt_____ sweater_____ jacket_____ shoes_____ belt__

blouse_____ skirt_____ slacks_____ dress_____ suit_____ coat_____

pajamas_____ robe_____ hat_____ gloves_____ ring_____

name ....

jeans_____ shirt_____ sweater_____ jacket_____ shoes_____ belt__

blouse_____ skirt_____ slacks_____ dress_____ suit_____ coat_____

pajamas_____ robe_____ hat_____ gloves_____ ring_____

name ....

jeans_____ shirt_____ sweater_____ jacket_____ shoes_____ belt__

blouse_____ skirt_____ slacks_____ dress_____ suit_____ coat_____

pajamas_____ robe_____ hat_____ gloves_____ ring_____

name ....

jeans_____ shirt_____ sweater_____ jacket_____ shoes_____ belt__

blouse_____ skirt_____ slacks_____ dress_____ suit_____ coat_____

pajamas_____ robe_____ hat_____ gloves_____ ring_____

name ....

jeans_____ shirt_____ sweater_____ jacket_____ shoes_____ belt__

blouse_____ skirt_____ slacks_____ dress_____ suit_____ coat_____

pajamas_____ robe_____ hat_____ gloves_____ ring_____

Christmas Card List

NAME	ADDRESS	SENT

Holiday MEMORIES

Hold on to priceless Christmas memories forever with
handwritten recollections of this season's magical moments.

Treasured Traditions

Keep track of your family's favorite holiday customs and pastimes on these lines.

....

....

....

....

....

....

....

....

....

....

....

....

....

Special Holiday Activities

What holiday events do you look forward to year after year? Write them down here.

....

....

....

....

....

....

....

....

Holiday Visits and Visitors

Keep a list of this year's holiday visitors. Jot down friend and family news as well.

....

....

....

....

....

....

....

....

....

....

....

....

....

....

....

....

....

....

....

....

....

....

This Year's Favorite Recipes

Appetizers and Beverages...

....

....

....

....

....

Entrées..

....

....

....

Sides and Salads...

....

....

....

Cookies and Candies..

....

....

....

....

Desserts...

....

....

LOOKING AHEAD

Holiday Wrap-up

Use this checklist to record thank you notes sent for holiday gifts and hospitality.

NAME	GIFT AND/OR EVENT	NOTE SENT
....	....	☐
....	....	☐
....	....	☐
....	....	☐
....	....	☐
....	....	☐
....	....	☐
....	....	☐
....	....	☐
....	....	☐
....	....	☐
....	....	☐
....	....	☐

Notes for Next Year

Write down your ideas for Christmas 2016 on the lines below.

....

....

....

....

....

....

....

....

....